THE IRISH PUB

JAMES FENNELL
AND
TURTLE BUNBURY

THE IRISH PUB

With 201 colour illustrations

Thames & Hudson

PAGE 2: *Morrissey's pub in Abbeyleix has been serving passers-by at least since the 1770s, when a lively shebeen existed on this site.*

THIS PAGE: *The Crown in Belfast, owned by the National Trust, is one of the finest examples of a Victorian saloon still in existence.*

For our friend Alex Davidson (1973–98) – 'Nosto Semper'.

And for our gorgeous daughters, Bella Fennell and Jemima Bunbury

First published in the United Kingdom in 2008 by Thames & Hudson Ltd, 181A High Holborn, London WC1V 7QX

www.thamesandhudson.com

© 2008 James Fennell and Turtle Bunbury

British Library Cataloguing-in-Publication Data
A catalogue record for this book is available from the British Library.

ISBN 978-0-500-51428-3

Printed and bound in China by Toppan Printing

Contents

Introduction

A cartoonesque Gross typewriter and sponge ball sculpture in P. J. Guerin are typical of the assorted oddities that abound in Irish bars.

THE IMPORTANCE OF THE PUB to community life in Ireland cannot easily be overstated. Whether by design or by accident, Irish pubs have become synonymous with free-flowing banter, fireside fiddles and unforgettable nights. They are perceived as places where friends and strangers happily chat, as sanctuaries where the soul is allowed a brief respite from gloomier realities. Indeed, the pub played such a vital role in the shaping of Ireland's once unshakably friendly and laid-back society that Irish pubs have been replicated in towns and cities across the planet.

According to the 12th-century Book of Leinster, the first feet to walk on Irish soil after the biblical Flood were those of a brewer and an innkeeper. Later, in the Middle Ages, Irish monks, starved of other forms of entertainment, wrote lengthy odes to beer. As the popularity of pilgrimages increased, so the monks began to offer ale and cider as well as accommodation and food. The first taverns were opened by the wine merchants who supplied the cellars of the Norman barons during the 13th century. These taverns rapidly became places of conversation, political debate and commercial transactions. In time, the inns and taverns would be joined by the countryside shebeens, illegal drinking dens famed for their evenings of immense revelry, dancing and hypnotic storytelling by wandering bards.

Thirty years ago, the pubs of Ireland were not much different to the shebeens of the 18th century. Before the sudden and unexpected boom of the 1990s, the Irish countryside was peppered with public houses where people of every class and creed gathered their senses and let them go again. Emboldened by drink, they swapped tales and jests, sang and shouted, shook hands and saluted, confessed and deceived, cackled and yawned, drank deep into the night and raised a glass to great men, beautiful women and their fathers who begat them. Giddy music and rattling tongues could light up the darkest corners and send young and old cavorting across the flagstone floors.

The purpose of this book is to celebrate, and document, pubs that epitomize that essential charm of old Ireland. The oldest pubs in the book date to the 17th century while the most recent was built from nothing in the late 1990s. As research, James and I journeyed through all thirty-two counties in Ireland, from the rocky coasts of

Morrissey's of Abbeyleix is one of many Irish pubs that simultaneously operated as a grocer.

the north to the mountains of the south, the boglands of the west to the urban sprawl of the east. Along the way we visited over seven hundred pubs from which we have chosen the thirty-nine whose stories appear in these pages.

Yet while our research was immensely good fun, it soon became clear that the classic Irish pub is an endangered species. For every pub that has closed in the past few years – and in recent times Irish pubs have been closing at the rate of one a day – a dozen more have been hurriedly 'modernized', with salt and pepper canisters on every table, homogenous fitted furniture and giant plasma screens blasting out sport and music. The entire pub experience has changed enormously. There are several reasons for this: the realities of the recent economic boom are too complex for most pubs to survive in their original form, while the ban on smoking in public places, combined with a crackdown on drink-driving, has brought a sad but necessary end to the more carefree attitude of days gone by. And since nearly every garage and newsagent in the country is now permitted to sell wine and beer, there has been a huge shift towards 'stay-at-home' drinking at every level of society. For the publican, there is a great temptation to sell the licence, often at considerable profit, to one of the insatiable pub chains or supermarkets stomping across the land. The upshot is that if you want to see what a traditional Irish bar looks like, you might have better luck in Chicago or Sydney than in Dublin, Galway or Tipperary.

The first section, 'Urban Retreat', examines some of the more metropolitan pubs that sprang up in the major cities during the 19th and early 20th centuries. Many of Dublin's pubs have a particularly dark and comfortable persona, perhaps derived from their proximity to the Guinness brewery. Belfast also has its share of characterful taverns, from The Crown (perhaps the most ornate bar in existence) to the more austere world of Kelly's Cellars. This chapter also embraces market-town bars, particularly those that doubled-up as hardware stores, shoe shops and undertakers.

The second section, 'Rural Charm', explores the more traditional country pub. Many of these

have also functioned as groceries, where patrons drank alongside tins of canned
fruit, reels of bailer twine and tubs of sheep dip. Such places are often replete with
snugs and back-bars where revolutions are plotted and romance ignites. Sadly the
number of grocery-bars has been declining for some time, and today there are
several counties where there are effectively none surviving. At the other extreme,
the countryside was dominated by simple, no-nonsense, one-room watering holes.
These are the pubs that are most under threat in the brave new world of 21st-century
Ireland. Lest we get too depressed, however, the third section, 'Contemporary
Heritage', lifts our spirits with four pubs, almost entirely created or recreated over
the past decade, that are judged to reflect the very best of Irish tradition. These pubs
prove that you don't need flashing television screens and ear-pounding sound
systems to draw a young, enthusiastic crowd.

Twenty-first-century Ireland is a multicultural, technologically advanced, cash-
hungry whirlpool. Many of the old institutions, such as the Catholic Church and
the Post Office, are struggling to retain their traditional place in communities.
The pub's best chance for survival is to adapt to the ever-changing needs of society,
without losing its essential charm. We hope this book will provide a chronicle of the
way things once were and remind us all of the enduring allure of the Irish pub.

Turtle Bunbury
A bar stool, Co. Monaghan

Urban Retreat

From the elaborate drinking halls of Victorian and Edwardian times to the more homely shop bars of the large market towns, urban dwellers have always enjoyed being just a short stroll away from at least one good pub. Dublin, Belfast and the other cities are all blessed with gorgeous and ever-popular drinking sanctuaries. For the market towns, change has been more noticeable — gone are the bantering farmers who once came for a drink after buying supplies or trading livestock. However, their bar stools have been filled by a new generation who still flock to these establishments for their unrivalled atmosphere of conviviality.

The Stag's Head, Dublin.

The Long Hall

This celebrated pub is a firm favourite with Dubliners

A convex mirror fitted to the top of an old whiskey cask creates a distorted reverse view of the bar.

ALTHOUGH THEY UNDOUBTEDLY mourned his passing in 1966 with genuine grief, for Patrick O'Brien's staff their loss was to some extent compensated by a remarkable gift: in his will, the octogenarian publican had left them his celebrated Victorian bar. However, a division soon emerged between the former bar staff with half wanting to sell and the other half wanting to keep the premises running. The bar duly went under the hammer and was purchased for £80,000 by Gerald Vincent Houlihan, who acquired much of the original contents at a further auction held on the premises.

Built by Lockwood and Mawson in 1877, The Long Hall occupies the ground level of a four-storey listed building on Dublin's South Great George's Street. Its red doors and red-and-white canopies have made the pub a landmark for many Dubliners. The pub looks across the street to 18th-century Georgian redbrick buildings, with the magnificent fairy-tale turrets and spires of George's Street Arcade to the north.

The Long Hall is the sort of place Isambard Kingdom Brunel would have created if he'd taken to pub design. The room is vast, reminiscent of a Victorian train station, its rich red-hued carpet split into two distinctive halves by an elaborate arched partition. The pub takes its name from a long hallway that apparently ran the length of the left-hand side of the building. Until 1951, the bar was men only but women sitting in this hallway were served through hatches. One of the regulars in this era was notorious Dublin bad boy playwright Brendan Behan, whose father worked across the road in Dockrells, the well-known hardware store.

Entering the bar, a line of aubergine-topped stools waits by the long, timber counter running along the right side. It was at this counter that Dublin rock legend Phil Lynott sank his stouts during the filming of the video to 'Old Town' in 1982. The back of the bar is a warren of deftly shaped baroque mirrors, fronted by shelves, glittering with pewter mugs, brandy glasses, bronze dishes and bottles. At the centre of the bar stands a mantel clock called 'Old Regulator', designed by the Frengley Brothers of Dublin, which confidently declares 'Correct Time'. On the wall, a short poem by Frank Holt called 'In Praise of Guinness' reads:

In Dublin there's a beauty that has no match,
It is brewed in St James's, then thrown down the hatch.

A ceiling of deep red embossed oak is bordered by deep and elaborate cornicing .
The lamps, all Victorian in style, come in different shapes and sizes – there are globe
lanterns, gleaming brass lamps and a miscellany of chandeliers over the bar.

The lounge and bar areas are separated
by an elaborate partition. A splendid
Wekler & Schlegel clock gives the
illusion of being in a Victorian train
station. The initials 'POB' are those
of the former owner, Patrick O'Brien.

The painting, by John Ward, RA, is from a series featuring famous bars from all over the world.

Elmwood bar stools invite one to watch the world roll by along South Great George's Street.

Halfway down the premises, an arched doorway, surmounted by an antique Wekler & Schlegel clock, marks the entrance to the main drinking lounge, originally oval-shaped and added to the original pub in about 1915. The lounge is a comfortable room, dimly lit by lanterns and the merry wisps of daylight that seep through a stained-glass window overhead. Along the left-hand wall hangs a series of prints called *The Criers of Dublin* (each focusing on a uniquely Irish object: a *Noddy or Chaise for two Persons*, or a *Hearse or Sedan used at Cork for people of Middling Station*); above, a pair of prints depict scenes from 19th-century Poland, bordered by antique single-barrelled muskets. On the right-hand wall, portraits of double-chinned Georgian women are juxtaposed with elaborate mirrors, a Jamaican rum barrel, an old letterbox and classical prints of orientals and deities. A charming grandfather clock patiently ticks to the right.

In the spacious lounge area, chairs gather along opposite walls like youngsters lining up for a jig. The walls are timber panelled for the most part; on these panels hang a series of framed prints of the Criers of Dublin, by Hugh Douglas Hamilton in the style of Francis Wheatley.

FOLLOWING PAGES: *The late 19th-century bar in The Long Hall runs some 15 metres (50 feet) down the right side of the room. Miscellaneous chandeliers, each set into its own unique rose, hang from a ceiling the colour of beetroot soup.*

The Stag's Head was completely rebuilt in 1895. The principal entrance features double columns of polished granite, with a canopy above and a unique oriel window springing out of an arched recess. Elaborate wrought-iron railings carry the initials of the pub's founder, George Tyson.

One of the original huge oak casks for storing whiskey, again bearing the founder's name.

The Stag's Head

DUBLIN CITY

Barristers, writers and students rub shoulders in this 19th-century landmark

Many tales are told as to the true origin of the eponymous stag, set beneath a richly panelled and moulded cornice.

'I DON'T THINK IT LOOKS LIKE A STAG', confesses bar manager John O'Toole. 'But he must have been a powerful big brute whatever he was.' The giant 14-pointer overlooking the bar certainly has a longer snout than the average stag. There are rumours that it was in fact a moose, dispatched in Alaska in 1901, but nobody's about to rename the place The Moose's Head. Tourists seem partial to the story that it was simply a runaway stag, destined for a dinner table in Dublin Castle, stopped only when it ran its head right into the original hostelry that stood here way back in the 1770s.

For some, the first indication that they are within range of The Stag's Head comes while strolling along the south side of Dame Street, away from Trinity College. A mosaic tile on the pavement depicts the noble head of a stag and points down a small alleyway, past the red-and-white pole of a barber shop. The present building was opened in October 1895, shortly after Dublin's wittiest playwright Oscar Wilde was sentenced to two years' hard labour. It was the brainchild of businessman George Tyson, who planned a pub that might bear 'favourable comparison with the best establishments of its kind either in London or in any other part of England'. Indeed, it was to be the first pub in Ireland to be electrified, controlled by a switchboard from behind the bar.

Designed by architect A. J. McLoughlin, the three-storey pub was built of Co. Dublin redbrick, with a façade of chiselled limestone, relieved by polished granite columns, sills and plinths. A polished granite frieze bears the pub's name in distinctive gold letters. Heavily moulded jambs and red granite pillars frame the main entrance, set beneath a canopy and an oriel window of Victorian bottle glass. Above the stag's head with gilded antlers over the entrance, is a clock on which Tyson's name is emblazoned. His initials echo along the wrought-iron railings beneath the pale green bay windows of the upper floors. Colourful flowers billow out of troughs and baskets along the wall.

The principal drinking area consists of a long, spacious room with a bar of polished mahogany, walnut and ebony running along the right-hand side. Dark oak whiskey casks are recessed into walls, complementing the richly panelled

Renaissance-style ceiling above. The eponymous stag springs everywhere – from mantel-shields, from the gable, from another mosaic at the back entrance and, above all, in the shape looming over the bar itself. While the original beer engines and nickel fittings have been replaced by a more contemporary bank of taps, the bowed counter is the same polished red Aberdeen granite installed by Tyson. The counter curls into a snug, once known as the Smoke Room, which occupies a one-storey return at the eastern end. Light floods in through six round-headed windows and is reflected throughout by bevelled mirrors deftly worked into the panelling.

Three large, dark oak whiskey casks are recessed into the back wall, harmonizing well with the surrounding dark wood.

For a pub to run smoothly, one needs unflappable bar staff and a manager who could double as a circus ringmaster. In that sense, The Stag's Head is amply served.

For John, the importance of service was drummed into him at an early age. His priorities are to keep the place as clean as possible and to ensure the beer that flows is of the highest quality. Guinness is their best-seller 'by a country mile', accounting for half of all pints sold. Wine is also on the increase. 'A few years ago a man wouldn't dare order a glass of wine in a pub', says John, 'but these days they're all at it.' There has also been a dramatic increase in women customers since the smoking ban. On the down side, they've lost the beer-swilling businessmen who would slip in at lunchtime for four or five pints. 'The smokers don't want to be seen standing outside', explains John.

The Stag's Head is a landmark in Dublin. Students from nearby Trinity College make up a sizeable portion of its customer base, while barristers, journalists and tourists are also frequently seen. The who's who of past drinkers includes James Joyce, Michael Collins and Quentin Tarantino. It also featured in the Wildean film, *A Man of No Importance*, starring Albert Finney. In 1978, The Stag's Head was purchased by the Shaffrey brothers of Bailieboro in Cavan. Peter Shaffrey was

Originally called the Smoke Room, the snug is a dark, comfortable sanctuary, the sense of space exaggerated by surrounding mirrors. The porch, windows and roof-lights are filled with heraldic stained glass, including more stag heads.

known to work sixty-hour weeks and would not get home until half past three in the morning. He felt that such an exhausting fate should not befall the next generation, and in July 2005 the Shaffreys sold the pub to the Louis Fitzgerald Group. This group owns a number of pubs in Dublin (including Kehoe's on South Anne Street and the Arlington Hotel on Bachelor's Walk), but The Stag's Head was a mighty trophy (complete with antlers). The beauty of this pub is that it is virtually unchanged since Tyson's day, and yet it has also jumped into the 21st century and landed firmly on all four feet.

Bermingham's

Everyone knows everyone else in this friendly pub

WITH A LICENCE DATING BACK TO 1884, Bermingham's is the oldest existing pub in Navan. It was built for a descendant of Robert de Bermingham, one of the warriors who accompanied 'Strongbow' (Richard de Clare) to Ireland during the momentous Anglo-Norman invasion. Patrick Bermingham was born in Dublin and apprenticed in the city's Broadstone Bar. In 1884, he moved north to Navan and purchased the two-room grocery-bar, returning to Dublin every week to collect fresh Guinness kegs from St James's Gate. The bar's interior, a Victorian treat, made his pub one of the most popular places in Meath's county town during the days when Navan's Great Leinster Fair, held every 14 November, was among the greatest agricultural shows in Europe. Navan was still a major centre of industry back then, with flax, flour, paper and oatmeal mills running the length of the river Boyne.

Patrick Bermingham did not long survive the opening of his new enterprise, passing away at the age of thirty-five. For the next sixty years his spinster sister, Jane Bermingham, ran the bar. Patrick's name remains above the bar today, proudly gilded on the exterior, framed by stone walls, wrought-iron rails and dark oak panelling. In 1917, Jane effectively adopted a five-year-old cousin, John Marmion, whose father was a veteran of the Boer War. John grew up in the pub, working behind the grocery counter from an early age. Upon Jane's death in 1948, he succeeded to the business.

A glass-fronted snug unfurls to the immediate left of the entrance. Three steps beyond stands the original grocery counter with the box drawers rising up the walls. To the right is a small open-plan space, where the wine cellar is kept in a glass-fronted cabinet. Along the walls are a sketch of Ludlow Street from 1985 and a photograph of John Marmion, clad in the white grocer's coat he sported for over sixty years until his death in 1985. Today the pub is owned and managed by his widow, Margaret (née Kerley), and son Michael.

An ornate railing surmounts the original tiled Victorian snug.

The bar runs along the left side with the old grocery counter at one end. Fixed upon on a wooden partition, a weather vane in the shape of a mounted horse leaps through the air, recalling a golden age, not so long ago, when the Navan and Fairy-house Races were so popular that both racetracks had their own railway stations. Michael Marmion maintains a personal interest in the horses, riding out for local trainers on a regular basis. The railway link with Dublin arrived in the 1850s and departed a century later, although somehow the GAA (Gaelic Athletic Association) manage to revive it for a weekend every time the Meath footballers make it to the All-Ireland finals in Dublin.

The ceiling is dominated by a riot of handsome brass pipes striding overhead. Although they look convincingly Victorian, Michael actually installed these in 1999 as part of a system to convert the nicotine-scented air into a pure, revitalizing breeze. Acoustic sessions take place in the back room, beneath a giant poster of a Guinness Extra Stout label, 'Bottled by P. Bermingham'. A series of rare advertisements are

The grocery counter and shelves were converted to bar use during the 1970s.

BELOW: *Bermingham's is home to many rare posters such as these for Power's whiskey and Jamaican rum.*

FACING PAGE: *Ceramic whiskey jars and bronze utensils from the early 20th century line an overhead shelf. The bar's wine collection is held in a glass-fronted cabinet on the wall.*

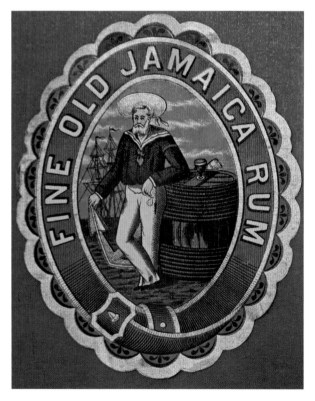

reflected in an enamel mirror – Cairness Drogheda Ales, Pimm's Double Ales ('Does You Double Good') and Bovril Biscuits. A shelf of ceramic pots and jars stands over a simple fireplace, stacked with logs in summer months. A poster for Watters Whiskey Pot Stills hangs alongside oil lamps, kettles and three handsome clocks ticking patiently against the back wall.

The oldest of these clocks dates to 1829, the year in which Ireland's beleaguered Catholic majority finally won the right to vote. Within a few months of the Catholic Emancipation Act, a child was born and he was called Patrick Bermingham.

Although educated in Navan, this was a different Patrick Bermingham to the eponymous publican. This Patrick was a latter-day Irish-Australian apostle who came to prominence in the late 1850s when, along with two fellow Irish Catholics, he attempted to depose the English Catholic hierarchy in Australia. To achieve his aims, Patrick gave extensive lectures in Italy and Ireland about how the vast infant colony down under was being run into the ground by useless English bishops and that good solid Irish bishops should be sent to the rescue without delay. Whether or not his accusations were just, Patrick was expelled from Australia in 1867.

Patrick Bermingham, the Australian apostle, is one of the names you might hear in Bermingham's pub today. Another Catholic of relevance was the recently beatified Blessed Columba Marmion (Joseph Aloysius Marmion), a kinsman of the present owner. Columba was twenty-eight years old when he abandoned his role as chaplain to a women's prison in Dublin and entered the Benedictine abbey at Maredsous in Belgium. Boasting an exceptional intellect, Columba was elected Abbot of Maredsous in 1909 and over the next fifteen years established the abbey as one of the great focal points for spiritual thinking in Europe. Maredsous was also famous worldwide for its excellent beer and pungent orange cheese, and perhaps some of that spirit permeated through the Marmion bloodline when John took the helm.

The Marmions open their pub from five o'clock every evening. 'Pubs are not the goldmines they once were, but if we get twenty people here, then the place is buzzing', says Michael. 'This place hasn't changed in ages', says old-timer Conor Walsh. 'Everyone knows everyone else, so it's very friendly. You never have a row here. It's a good pub, the best in town.'

Clancy's

That rare thing: a pub where music and sport complement one another

ON 2 JULY 1903, TWELVE MOTORCARS came hurtling through the narrow streets of Athy in the closing stages of the Gordon Bennett Cup, a precursor of the modern Grand Prix. Among those who watched the Belgian 'Red Devil' Camille Jenatzy thunder towards victory may well have been William Scully, a 38-year-old businessman from Timahoe who had opened a grocery-bar on the town's Leinster Street earlier that year. Perhaps, as the clouds of smoke dissipated, he turned to his Galway-born fiancée, Mary Finucane, and wondered aloud at this ever-changing world.

A few miles away, in Stradbally, Mrs Mary Shortall may also have watched the passing of the motorcars. She might even have allowed her two small nephews, Jim and Michael Clancy, to sneak a glance. Their parents, John and Kate Clancy, hailed from the coal-mining terrain of Clogh in Co. Kilkenny but had died of pneumonia within nine days of each other in October 1893.

Shortly after Mary Shortall's death in 1908, young Jim Clancy secured a job as a shop assistant in William and Mary Scully's pub. By 1911, the eighteen-year-old was packing boxes of soap, sugar and tea for the cloth-capped customers. After William Scully's death in 1938, Jim purchased the pub from William's widow. Jim ran the pub with his wife, Maureen, for nearly forty years until his death in 1976. As a mark of respect to his mentor, the name above the door remained 'William Scully' until the end of the Second World War, when it was changed to 'Clancy'. And that's what it's been ever since.

It seems somehow astonishing that Ger Clancy, the sprightly gentleman who now runs that same grocery-bar, is the son of Jim Clancy, born in 1893. But history is forever playing tricks with time. Ger was involved with the pub from an early age but managed to escape to America in his youth, when he had dreams of becoming both an accounting millionaire and an international rugby player. Ger came back to help run the pub shortly before his mother's death in 1996. He has been running the show with his wife, Breda, ever since.

Ger is a passionate fan of the old-style Irish bar. As such, he and Breda have done much to bring the pub back to its original Edwardian state. The exterior was

Photographs of past drinkers at Clancy's fill every wall.

repainted in the traditional combination of signal red, black and white. Assisted by Eddie Rice, Ger stripped the panelling and bar of all its paint, save for a useful red Formica sheet on the bar counter. They then varnished the entirety with a black Burmese teak finish. A floor of Chinese slate was laid over the old cracked tiles. William Scully's original grocery shelves remain in position although that aspect of the business faded out after Jim's death. The old ledgers rest beside a vintage railway lamp presented to Ger by his father-in-law. Car registration plates collected by Ger from every one of the United States are juxtaposed with photographs of heroic sportsmen, folk musicians and beloved patrons past. On other walls hang newspaper clippings, playbills for the abandoned Grove Cinema, old posters for snuff and

ABOVE LEFT: *A Singer sewing-machine table stands on a slate floor. The back wall is festooned with photographs of local sporting and musical heroes from the past half-century.*

ABOVE: *Like many Irish pubs, Clancy's bottled their own Guinness until the 1970s.*

The original grocery section has been converted into an L-shaped bar. The box drawers above formerly contained spices and tobacco.

Woodbines. Along a spacious corridor painted in a retro diamond fashion by artist Paul Hughes, hangs an ancient rattle, last wound up to maximum effect when Kildare won the All-Ireland Senior Football Championship in 1928. The beer garden incorporates the old bottling area and stable yard where traders kept wool supplies back when Athy was the largest market town in the area.

Thom's Directory of 1926 records forty-one 'wine and spirit dealers' in Athy. By 2007, that number had fallen to sixteen. To stay afloat you need to be different and that is where Clancy's has a trump card. In 1964, Jim Clancy evicted all the dusty old bags of maize from the grocery's storeroom and reopened it as a music room. Nearly fifty years later, Clancy's is considered one of the great music pubs of eastern Ireland. The weekly 'seisun' now takes place in the old sitting room where Jim and his card-playing friends used to play 'twenty-five' (Ireland's national card game) from half nine in the morning. Ger remembers being regularly summoned to this room as a boy and dispatched to the bookies across the road to back a horse. Every Thursday night, somewhere between twelve and fifteen musicians now congregate here. They play fiddles, bodhráns, flutes and mandolins, and sing songs about long-gone tyrants, rising moons and rose-peppered valleys. 'A lot of the older people live for Thursday night', says Ger. 'We've lost a good few of the older guys who used to play in the last five years but we have plenty of new players to keep it going.' The tobacco-stained walls are pasted with scores from songbooks, classical and traditional. The audience sway upon scruffy benches and assorted chairs, tapping their heels on the wide-plank floor and allowing their voices to join in with the repetition of each rousing chorus. Many have heard about these nights and travelled from a considerable distance. The sound of music occasionally rebounds off oil lamps, a Superser heater and dark overhead rafters and reels into the rest of the pub via a useful hatch made from the timber of old school desks.

Clancy's is that rare pub where music and sport complement one another. 'It was always a sporting pub', says Ger who captained the Kildare Minors when beaten by Tyrone in the 1973 All-Ireland final at Croke Park. Originally it focused on the GAA sports of hurling and Gaelic football, but with Ger an avid rugby player, that brought in a rugby crowd too. Horse racing is also a regular feature. 'And now since we've all got too old to play sport, its gone to golf.' The pub's team is the Loose Porter Golf Society, named for an expression Ger heard an old man use for draft beer: 'It's loose in the keg as opposed to bottled', he said.

The owner has collected number plates from every state in the USA. Some are hung above the hawthorn honey made in Ballycolla by his octogenarian father-in-law, Tommy Maher.

Ger is unconvinced that any of his four teenage daughters will take on the pub. 'Being brought up in a pub is like being brought up with bees. You run away from it. When they were young, they enjoyed it. But how can you study for your exams with this racket up above? To make life easier for them all, Ger relocated his family to the outskirts of town in the spring of 2007.

E. J. Morrissey's

ABBEYLEIX – CO. LAOIS

A pub of legendary charm, packed with reminders of the old world

Among the many photographs that hang on the walls are these two, showing Morrissey's staff in 1892 and again in the 1920s.

FACING PAGE: *Since the earliest days, all staff at Morrissey's have worn the white coats of the grocer.*

IN MORE CAREFREE TIMES, THERE was an unofficial commandment that stated: 'Thou shalt not drive through Abbeyleix without pausing in Morrissey's for a pint.' Considering Abbeyleix's beguiling location on the main Dublin–Cork road, this law firmly established the premises as an institution of major importance.

The pub's origins stem back to 1775 when local landowner Thomas Vesey effectively founded the town by allocating property rights to his tenants. Within a year, Vesey had been awarded a Viscountcy and a single-storey house was built on the site where Morrissey's stands today. During the following century, a swinging shebeen operated here, with a reputation that stretched far beyond the humble bounds of Abbeyleix.

The present building was commissioned in 1875 by Edward Morrissey, grandfather of the legendary William J. Morrissey who ran the premises from the mid-1920s until his death in 1982. Known as Willie Joe, the younger Morrissey was a famous character in Irish folklore. He was the town rep for the Cunard Line in an age when the Abbeyleix Carpet Factory kitted out the *Titanic* with its elaborate rugs and carpets. Although loath to admit it, Willie Joe was so deaf that one effectively had to order a drink with a pen and paper.

If his hearing was impaired, his sixth sense benefited accordingly. Murray Anderson was one of the men who bottled the wine for Morrissey's. The story goes that the aroma got to him and he took two bottles, wedging them deep into his coat pockets. Murray was making his way out the door when Willie Joe offered him a pint. The bottler declined, saying he was not feeling the best. Willie Joe urged the man to sit tight by the fire and warm himself. Murray reluctantly obliged. Before long the heat from the fire caused both bottles to explode in his jacket. Murray may have been drenched and somewhat embarrassed but it didn't stop him from fathering twenty-three children.

When Willie Joe died aged eighty-seven, the pub passed to his cousin, P. J. Mulhall, a sprightly elfin man and everyman jack who, as well as being a tea, wine and spirit merchant, was district manager of the local First National Building Society, an auctioneer, a 100-acre farmer and head of the local tourist industry. Perhaps anticipating that such a workload might be the end of him, Mulhall was also the local undertaker, escorting hearses to and from the surrounding graveyards on the back of a beautiful two-seater Victorian pony-trap. P. J. died in 2004 and the pub was sold to Carlow publican Tom Lennon who has thankfully retained the pub's traditional interior right down to the official white grocery coats sported by the bar staff.

The pub is effectively a large wooden cavern, softly lit by lamps that hang from a ceiling held up by metal beams. The room is loosely carved into a warren of snugs and seating areas by dint of wooden partitions and stand-alone walls seemingly crafted from old biscuit tin lids and dismantled clocks. The legendary charm of Morrissey's undoubtedly hails from the incredible collection of old-world goods on display on its dark shelf-lined walls. These shelves are packed with the sort of products that would have abounded in a village grocery half a century ago: huge jars of sweets, an old slicing machine, an Edwardian cash register, a tin of Bourneville cocoa from the Boer War, Boyne Valley corn flakes, packets of freshly ground coffee and Morrissey's own 'Famous Tea', right beside the scales on which the packs were weighed. The walls are bedecked with wonderful advertisements from the early 20th century. 'Hello Daddy! Guess What I've Just Got!', says a happy girl with a Fry's chocolate bar in her hand, while two cloth-capped flappers motoring through the countryside, smoking furiously, hatch down, appear beneath the teasing caption, 'Gold Flake – The Man's Cigarette that Women Like'.

In its heyday, Morrissey's was one of the pioneering establishments where barmen received their training. In the sort of initiative one would expect certain low-budget airlines to adopt, the apprentices often paid the pub for the privilege of working there. An apprentice spent his first year working behind the bar before graduating to the grocery section. Training for bar-work was considerably more specialized in

those days. One had to be able to bottle beer, decanting each one so that the sediment stayed behind. Pouring a pint was a serious work of art. Whiskey also came in large containers and had to be 'tested' for 'specific gravity'. Apparently, the railway staff who transported the drink south were partial to sampling the containers, then refilling with water. The rule of thumb was that the further you were from Dublin, the more your whiskey was watered. But the railway men never watered Morrissey's whiskey – they knew it was always tested.

A wall of biscuit-tin lids greets the drinker, recalling such beloved classics as Geary's Thin Arrowroot and Jacob's Marietta.

FACING PAGE: Balanced upon grocery drawers, giant jars offer clove rock, cola cubes, lemon bonbons, butter nuggets and succulent chocolate satins.

Lenehan's

The sort of pub that's busy on a Monday morning for no particular reason

The Lenehan family has run the Kilkenny pub since the end of the First World War.

'YOU MIGHT SAY IT'S ALL ABOUT THIRTY-THREE', says Jim Lenehan. 'I was born in 1933. Kilkenny beat Limerick in the All-Ireland in 1933. And it's thirty-three yards in a single run from this end of the bar to the other.'

The building in which Jim Lenehan lives and runs his bar has stood here for at least two hundred years, though the name of its original publican is unknown. In the late 1890s, Laurence Long, a tea, wine and spirit merchant from Co. Tipperary, set up shop in the building, securing a market that included the employees of the gasworks and soldiers from the British infantry barracks on Ballybough Street. Jim produces a photograph of a garrison on parade just outside the pub in 1899. Weeks later, they sailed for South Africa where scores of them were killed, wounded and captured in the bloody Battle of Colenso.

In Laurence Long's day, Jim's grandparents, Dan and Rose Lenehan, ran another pub, the Kilkenny House (now called O'Gorman's) on John Street. In 1911, they purchased Long's pub at 10 Barrack Street for their son William. William married

FACING PAGE: Invoice dockets and curling brown bills from the pub's early days are among the memorabilia kept inside a glass cabinet.

Leather stools and tobacco-stained walls, combined with creaky shelves, give the illusion that one has stepped into the 1950s.

Catherine Hogan in the early 1920s and Jim is their son.

Lenehan's is the sort of pub that becomes extremely busy on a Monday morning for no particular reason. Both Jim and his wife, Carmel, are fourth generation publicans so they are sure to have inherited a few trade secrets along the way. Today, their long, wooden-panelled interior offers customers a welcome respite from the escalating mayhem of the streets outside. Awaiting your drink, you can lose yourself browsing a wall covered in old advertising posters – Clarke's Plug, Player's Navy Cut, Quaker Oats, O'Connell's Dublin Ale, Corcoran & Co of Carlow, St Bruno Flake, Smithwick's Ale, Lambs Brother Jam and Burma Sauce (with the immortal caption, 'The Only "Sauce" I Dare Give Father').

Elsewhere, shelves are festooned with antique National typewriters, ceramic chamber pots, sooty calendars and photographs of the ever-victorious Kilkenny Cats, Ireland's most successful hurling team. 'I did a bit of hurling myself', admits Jim. 'Got myself a few broken noses and so on.' A crackling log fire is reflected in a massive Lambert & Butler mirror, while roughshod chairs and sturdy stools stretch along the black mahogany bar into the old bottling room, where light lunches of soup and sandwiches are now served. Behind the bar, barrel tops set into sagging shelves proclaim, 'Whiskey', 'Port' and 'Brandy'.

In 1925, the Lenehans renovated the building by rearranging rooms, laying flagstone floors (since tiled), adding a pitch pine ceiling and rebuilding some of the walls with a concoction of brick, lime and horsehair. They also installed coal chutes and a range cooker. Many relics survive, including the spice and herb drawers and the graceful bins where Laurence Long kept his tea, flour and oatmeal.

The Lenehans were always good at diversity, aided by a small farm to the rear of the pub. During the Second World War – or the Emergency as it was called in neutral Ireland – the pub enjoyed a bountiful export of poultry and rabbits to Billingsgate Market in London. Cattle were also lucrative, particularly after the Kilkenny Mart opened at Christmas 1956, just a few hundred metres from the pub.

The cattle mart has since been sold to Tesco and the farmers now do their business in a new market in the suburbs. This has inevitably had major repercussions on the farming populace who once frequented Lenehan's. 'We're in the middle of mighty changes', says Jim. 'We used to have five and thirty farmers drinking here, waiting for their lot number to be called.' The pub still derives good business from teachers, nurses and clergy in the locality, as well as the soldiers in the barracks and workers from the Labour Exchange. Jim likes the fact they are off the beaten track. They have the hurling grounds of Nowlan Park around the corner and that ensures plenty of trade. 'Next Sunday we'll be buried in people because of the hurling', he predicts.

Classic advertising posters from the 1930s and 1940s adorn every wall.

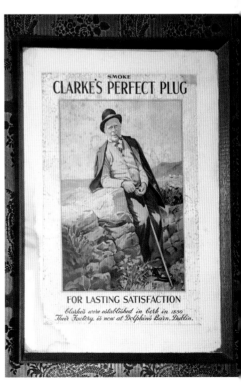

McCarthy's

For many in the horse-racing crowd, it's really not a long way to Tipperary

Traditionally the snugs either side of the main entrance allowed women to drink in peace while the menfolk discussed menfolk matters in the main bar.

FACING PAGE: *McCarthy's commendable attention to detail extends to a handsome bank of bronze and enamel taps along the bar.*

WHEN THE AUTHOR OF *Guy's Postal Directory of Munster, 1886*, came to compile his section on the Co. Tipperary market town of Fethard, he can't have failed to notice the name of Michael McCarthy. From a single building on Main Street, this enterprising citizen was listed as baker, china and glass dealer, linen and woollen draper, grocer and spirit dealer, vintner and, perhaps most tellingly, town commissioner. Michael McCarthy died just five years later at the age of sixty-four.

He had come a long way since his arrival in Fethard from a farm in the Comeragh Mountains beyond. Exactly when he arrived is unknown. He was not registered in 1846 but had a grocery in 1856 and was among those who signed the Cormack petition of 1858, calling for a review of the criminal justice system in Ireland.

Fethard (pronounced 'Feathered') stands in the middle of a beautiful, undulating plain of smoky mountains and wet roads, co-ops and creameries, ruined monasteries and lean racetracks. It became a town of consequence in the 13th century when encircled by a wall that still stands proud today, restored in the past few years. Cromwell's army camped here in the 1640s and the British army set up a barracks in the town in 1805. By then, Fethard's predominant business involved supplying the surrounding countryside with everyday goods. It also hosted a market every Monday and had five annual fair days. Bianconi's coaches (see p. 127) frequently passed through the town on their way to Dublin and, later in the century, three trains arrived daily, *en route* from Clonmel to Thurles.

When Michael McCarthy's widow, Mary, died in 1897, her eldest son, Richard, took the helm. In the 1886 directory, Richard was listed as a 'Boot and Shoe Maker'. In his short tenure as head of the family, he converted the shop on Main Street into one of the most popular hotels in Tipperary, operating thirty livery stables and a hackney-carriage service from a series of yards running along the old town wall. Much of his business came from the nearby garrison and the cattle drovers who arrived at night to attend the monthly fairs. By seven in the morning all transactions were complete, the livestock was on the train to Dublin and everyone was ready for some good food and drink. Richard McCarthy made sure his hotel attracted its share of the business, with his staff preparing bacon and cabbage from half three in the afternoon.

Now groaning with wine bottles, the original grocery shelves are partially hidden behind a timber and stained-glass snug.

Richard died in 1911, aged fifty-two. For the next thirty years, Richard's widow, Mary, mother of his thirteen children, ran the business. The children were famous characters in the locality. One son, Gus McCarthy, a prominent Gaelic footballer, was playing for Tipperary at Croke Park when British forces opened fire on the crowd on Bloody Sunday, 1920. His team-mate Mick Hogan was among the fifteen killed that afternoon. While Gus served with the Irish Republican Army, his brother Chris was a veteran of the British Crown forces and served in the trenches during the First World War. Chris later won the four-mile Conyngham Cup, then the centrepiece of the Punchestown festival.

Some years ago, a nun from Fethard was sipping tea with a friend in Pietermaritzburg, South Africa, when an elderly gentleman approached and asked where they were from. When the nun explained that her home was Fethard, the gentleman revealed that, as a young officer in the British Army, he had been stationed in the Fethard barracks during the Irish War of Independence. One of his duties had

been to go to McCarthy's Hotel and personally deliver secret missives to Michael Collins, then Director of Intelligence for the Irish Republican Army.

A third McCarthy brother, Dick, born in 1905, was the grandfather of Jasper Murphy who runs the pub today. Dick was a keen hurler, footballer and boxer, but also excelled in the 'foreign sports', playing scrum half for Fethard one minute and taking to the cricket crease at Derryluskin the next. However, it was as a National Hunt jockey that Dick McCarthy was best known. In 1929, he went to Bob Gore's stables at Findon in Sussex where, in his first season, he rode seventeen winners and came second in the Cheltenham Gold Cup. Dick spent twenty-two years in the saddle competing on racetracks across the British Isles, including three cracks at the Aintree Grand National.

After Mary McCarthy's death in 1943, the two-storey hotel passed to her bachelor son Jack. Dick frequented the pub but wanted nothing to do with the running of it. 'You could be giving drink to a fellow half the night and you could be giving it to him

The rough and ready ambience of McCarthy's has made it a huge favourite with Ireland's horse-racing enthusiasts.

for nothing and in the finish he would turn around and abuse you.' Dick's sisters, Beattie, Kitty and Nellie, were also given life use of the premises. When Jack died in 1967, the sisters closed the hotel, concentrating instead on the pub. Upon Betty's death in 1978, the operation passed to Dick's daughter, Annette.

By day the banter in McCarthy's is dominated by the conundrums of the dairy industry and the cryptic world of horse racing. The pub is the spiritual home of Coolmore Stud, the most successful thoroughbred stud in the world. A number of outstanding stables are also to be found in the vicinity. Numerous well-known faces have been spotted here over the years; Andrew Lloyd Webber lives nearby and it was here that he and Ben Elton wrote the musical *The Beautiful Game*.

McCarthy's possesses a dark and inviting interior, its tobacco-stained walls smothered by images of men clutching trophies, well-toned horses in mid-flight, revolutionaries at play, the Bloody Sunday football team. The art includes prints of stags and pheasants and an atmospheric portrait by Peter Curling. The grocery shelves lie to the left, partially screened by a stained-glass snug and advertisements for Fry's chocolate. Rattan stools wait along a counter of solid oak that runs the

length of the right-hand wall, broken midway by an arch. As one passes into a wider area, with comfortable sofas and a curiously ornate Emperor stove on the left, the soft light vanishes into the panelling on the walls and ceiling above. It remerges to the rear where a door points the way to a restaurant.

McCarthy's has a catchphrase: 'We wine you, dine you and bury you.' Sure enough, the pub offers both an up-market restaurant and an acclaimed undertaker service. Coffins and hearses are parked in the former livery stables out the back. Annette's son Jasper has enjoyed this side of the business ever since their ancient hearse driver greeted him with the immortal words, 'I was dead for a while when you were away'. Jasper began undertaking when he was thirteen. 'I was thrown into it, lifting bodies and all that.' As such, he is aware of the old superstitions of Fethard that the deceased should never pass through the street where Cromwell allegedly slipped from his horse and cursed the ground. The McCarthys have some spiritual superstitions of their own. When a family member is close to death, it is said that a picture falls from a wall, followed by three loud knocks at the front door. Jasper lives nearby with his New Zealand-born wife, Sarah, and their two children. After fifteen years away, he has happily 'melted back into the place' where he splits his time between running the business and his private passions of flying airplanes and researching local history.

The Bulman

A nautical pub where the television goes on only for Irish hurling

AS THE AUTUMN OF 1601 FADED into winter, a fleet of ships carrying some four thousand Spaniards docked at Kinsale on the south coast of Co. Cork. Their plan was to unite with the Ulster chieftains O'Neill and O'Donnell, and oust the invading English army from Ireland's shores for once and for all. Unfortunately for the Spanish, Kinsale is situated about as far away from Ulster as you can get. In an early example of rapid response, the English swiftly surrounded Kinsale and laid siege to the Spanish. The Ulster chieftains gamely attempted a rescue, leading their armies on a colossal march south through the centre of Ireland. On Christmas Eve, 1601, the Spanish and Irish forces attempted to lift the siege. Their defeat was inevitable, bloody and calamitous. O'Neill and O'Donnell surrendered and, in due course, fled the country. Their exodus signalled the end of Gaelic Ireland.

When the Spanish commander, Don Juan d'Aquila, first landed at Kinsale, he and his officers were given refuge amid the stony walls of Ringcurran Castle by Barry Og, Baron of Kinalea. Barry Og's fate after the battle is unknown but his castle was flattened in the 1670s to make way for Charles Fort, one of the most formidable defensive fortresses on the Irish coast.

In 1820, Barry Og's direct descendant Catherine Barry established herself as a publican just a stone's throw from the family's former headquarters. Her own descendant, Aidan Barry, believes a pub has stood on the site since the 16th century. Certainly, the fine coastal location would have merited pause for refreshment from the earliest times. In Catherine's day, with the Napoleonic Wars still a recent memory, Charles Fort had 100 mounted brass cannon pointing out to sea. All vessels passing up the harbour were within a pistol shot of its battery. A good deal of the pub's trade came from the various regiments garrisoned in the fort. By the late 19th century, it had become an unofficial mess, while officers of higher rank often attended musical evenings in the Barry family drawing room upstairs. The pub was known as 'The Thatch', on account of its roof, until 1899 when Catherine's grandson, Patrick Barry, replaced the original pub with the present building, and named it 'Barry's'.

When the RMS *Lusitania* was sunk by a German U-boat in 1915, rescue efforts were co-ordinated out of Kinsale. In time Barry's would become the establishment

The Bulman is named for a merchant ship that sank in Kinsale harbour during the 19th century.

The Barry family's original hearth now warms those gathered to hear live music four nights a week.

of choice for the celebrated 'rocket team' coastguards, so named for their tactic of firing rockets, with hooks and ropes attached, at distressed boats, which they could then pull to safety.

During the 1960s, the pub passed from Patrick's grandson, Daniel Joseph Barry, to his three sons, Aidan, Pat and Donal. In 1969, the Barry brothers renamed the pub 'The Bulman' after the Bulman Buoy, a well-known nautical landmark, which directs boats to safe entrance into the harbour. The buoy was named for a merchant ship called *The Bulman*, which ran aground on the rocks with all hands lost. The Earl Mountcashell's yacht was also wrecked on the Bulman rock in 1846.

In 1976, the Barry brothers sold the pub to a local couple, Willie and Kaye O'Brien, who ran it for thirteen years, living with their two children in rooms above the bar. During the early 1990s, the new owners, Chris and Lorrie Agar, converted the

No nautical pub is complete without a ship's cat – this one is called Rusty.

former living quarters into a restaurant. The pub then passed from Fergus Sheridan to Oliver Flynn, under whom it received the last ever Black and White Pub of the Year Award in 2004. The following spring, the pub was sold to the present owners, Gerard and Margaret Gannon, who completely renovated it. 'The entire place was stripped, sanded, varnished and painted', says manager Conor Ryan. 'Everything was carefully photographed beforehand and put back exactly where it was.'

Full-length portraits of O'Neill and d'Aquila stand solemnly beneath flower baskets by the main entrance. Light tumbles in from the ocean, and heat rises from fireplaces in rooms at either side. The bar counter is pitched at the perfect height for old men to lean upon, while colourful tiles salvaged from Catherine Barry's original bar form a border around the base, yielding to Chinese slate on the wider floor. The bar is amply stocked with Cork's well-known refreshments – Cork Dry Gin, Middleton whiskey, Beamish Stout and the increasingly popular Kinsale Irish Lager.

An hourly gong resounds from an eight-day clock made by J. Hillser & Sons of Cork. A *Titanic* made from lollipop sticks is docked behind the bar. A bronze-hued ceiling features sculptured birds and giant hands by Don Meaney, alongside telescopes and anchors. Hanging like a drying rail above the bar, oars salvaged from the Summercove slipway have been converted into an overhead light.

The Bulman is at heart a mariner's pub. An Evershed & Vignoles transmitter from 1959 suggests 'Full Steam Ahead'. Elsewhere, a Victorian sextant by Joseph Moore stands alongside four of Guillaume Blaeu's extraordinarily accurate copper-etched maps of the New World from the 1630s. Portraits of cloth-capped drinkers from times past hang alongside other frequenters such as the late Taoiseach (prime minister), Charles J. Haughey. One particularly hardy Irish-Italian fisherman could apparently drink thirty pints a day and certainly looked eighty by the age of fifty.

To the right of the bar is a small room of parquet floor, timber walls and ripped leather, known as 'Miah's Room'. Drinkers recline in colonial armchairs, lately reupholstered, surrounded by tongue-and-groove walls with old hessian rope carefully placed between each plank to create a nautical effect. Mighty beams traverse the bronze-tinted ceiling above. Where one might expect a fan in a more tropical country, three dolphins circle a rudder crafted into lights, again by Don Meaney. Along the walls hang a Lifebuoy soap advertisement from 1900, a map showing the lighthouses of the locality lit up, and miscellaneous paintings and photographs of sailing vessels, lobster pots and fishing nets.

To the left of the bar, an archway leads through to the music room, combining the original hallway and a family bedroom. Adjacent to a large granite fireplace, a grand piano from G. A. Buckland & Co. acts as the focal point for round-table sessions Wednesday through Saturday. 'Everyone expects bars along the coast here to have music', says Conor. A television is discreetly tucked away in a dark corner, hidden by old ropes and bits of sack so you barely notice it. 'The TV never goes on, except for hurling or football on a Sunday', insists Conor.

The windows of The Bulman give on to the waters of Summercove and the khaki headland beyond. The English fort still stands stern on the green terrain where the siege of Kinsale took place four centuries ago. This fine spectacle is well known to the thousands who gather here in summer months to sip cold beers in the sunshine, bare feet swinging over the pier below. When night falls, The Bulman enters a new phase as candlelight and flickering fires rearrange themselves to suit the rumbling banter along the bar and merry patrons kick a heel to the rhythm of the dancing fiddles. From the blustery beyond comes the smell of the high seas and of the powerful history of this small piece of land.

The main bar counter was stripped of emulsion in the 2005 renovation. Nautical memorabilia abounds on ceiling and walls.

Dick Mack's

A cracking good pub, still full of reminders of its shoe-making past

FACING PAGE: The owner of Dick Mack's, Oliver J. MacDonnell, was born in one of the upstairs rooms and has been based in the pub ever since.

The MacDonnells' kitchen was opened as an alternative room in the 1990s. The artist Jay Killian is depicted at play on the pub's Schiedmayer piano.

'A LOT OF PEOPLE THINK I WAS NAMED for Oliver Reed but it was actually for the Blessed Oliver Plunkett [the martyred Primate of All Ireland]', explains dapper Kerry publican, Oliver Joseph Mary MacDonnell. Oliver was the (slightly) older of twin boys born to Dick and Angela MacDonnell in 1951. His twin runs a farm the far side of the Conor Pass. When Dick died in 1992, Oliver took on the pub. Not because he was the eldest but 'because I worked the hardest at it', he says with a wry smile.

The MacDonnells have been in Dingle since at least the 1700s. Oliver's grandfather, Tom MacDonnell, was born at the height of the Great Famine in 1848. When the Tralee and Dingle Light Railway and Tramway opened in 1891, Tom was appointed Station Master. His role was to choreograph the passage of all goods, cattle and passengers on this, the most westerly railway line in Europe. In 1899, Tom Mack branched out, opening a grocery and general store on Dingle's Green Street. The tea, flour and sugar bins he installed are still there today, stamped with the MacDonnell crest and their adopted motto, 'As You Like It'.

When Dick succeeded to the pub in 1938, he promptly established himself as the town's foremost boot merchant. Down the line came the first consignments of Wellingtons from the Hunter factory in Scotland, closely followed by shoes from the Mullan shoe factory in Co. Monaghan. Today, the dominant feature in Dick Mack's pub is the timber shelving rising from floor to ceiling on two of the three principal walls. Each shelf is stacked to the brim with tobacco-stained shoeboxes, rubber boots, leather shoes, floppy runners, boxes of buckles and trimmings of old tawny leather. At its peak, Dick and two apprentices operated a shoe-repair business; the leather-making tools they used are still on site. He also specialized in belts, which, says Oliver, tugging at his own, was a particularly thrifty business. Nail boots were another success. 'They were hard-wearing, and the nails made them perfect for climbing the mountains.'

The shelves above Tom Mack's original tea bins are stacked with tobacco-stained boxes, odd shoes and a portrait of the late Irish Taoiseach, Charles J. Haughey.

The railway was always an enigma. It brought many strangers to Dingle. But it took a lot of people away, many of whom never came back. Dingle's émigrés tended to settle in Boston. Three of Oliver's aunts left for London and rarely returned home thereafter. When the railway closed in 1953, the mood was sombre. Oliver's godfather, J. J. O'Connor, was one of the biggest cattle dealers in Ireland at the time and frequently dispatched his herds by train to Dublin. That said, his godson raised no objections. 'My mother told me I cried all the way down from Dublin because I couldn't stand the noise of it.'

When arthritis got the better of Dick in the 1970s, he left young Oliver to look after the pints and to bottle the beer. Dick retired behind the counter to repair shoes, cut lengths for belts and fit some of the new buckles that had come in from Walsall near Birmingham in England. By the 1980s, cheaper imports from Asia and rising labour costs prompted Dick to call it a day on the shoe front. But, where others might have disposed of all remaining footwear in a bin, Dick simply left them exactly where they were and carried on with the pub. Likewise, to the eternal gratitude of innumerable newcomers to Dingle over the past twenty years, Dick's son has kept it all precisely as it was. But Oliver was by no means an idle publican. He was one of the first to start selling wine in the town and, before long, was offering thirty-two different varieties of French wine, acquired from Lee White & Company in Cork.

Tourism has been a mainstay of Dingle's economy ever since *Ryan's Daughter* was filmed on the peninsula in 1968. Oliver recalls serving Robert Mitchum the occasional brandy between the actor's guest-house romps. Capitalizing on Dingle's new-found love affair with Hollywood, Dick duly started his own 'Walk of Fame' on the street outside the pub's red front door. The first pair to be immortalized in stars were two Kerrymen – Antarctic explorer Tom Crean and writer Jerome O'Connor. The honour has since been bestowed upon a dozen more, including Sir John Mills, who played the village mute in *Ryan's Daughter*, and Dolly Parton, who celebrated by sitting on the counter. 'A lot of people think she's a big woman', confides Oliver. 'But I can assure you that, while she's all there, she's really very small.'

In 1984, a friendly dolphin called Fungie pirouetted into the plot and Dingle experienced another wave of publicity. With annual visitors now touching quarter of a million, locals are inevitably

divided as to the benefits of tourism. The town is certainly one of the liveliest on the west coast of Ireland but some of the older generation perhaps struggle to reconcile this with the Dingle of their youth. Along the walls of Dick Mack's pub are early 20th-century photographs suggesting a town of muddy streets and open drains, overrun with donkeys and carts, old women in black shawls carrying baskets, rugged men in cloth caps and skinny children in bare feet. It's hard to believe this is the same town that lights the night sky with such determination in the 21st century.

Dick Mack died in 1992 and his wife followed eight months later. 'She said she'd never marry a fellow with a hole in his jumper but she did', says her son. Oliver has run the show ever since, aided and abetted by his wife, Josephine. By a strange coincidence, she too is a twin. He does not expect any of his three daughters to take on the premises but, as he says, who knows? He kept his father's name above the door because Oliver is a modest man and, while he was born and raised in the building, he and his family now live out of town. He has converted the old family kitchen, sitting and dining areas into alternative drinking spots for his customers. He still enjoys the pub business but is equally at home tending to the few cows

The grocery shelves behind the main tongue-and-groove bar are abundantly stocked with bottles from across the world. The Garryowen Plug advertisement was salvaged from a bog near Cloghane.

he keeps on a nearby farm. Although he endeavours to open the pub every morning personally, he no longer works at night. 'I did thirty-five years of nights', he says with feeling.

Dick Mack's is a cracking good pub. There aren't many like it left. By night it seems as though every rattan stool, bentwood chair and scuff-resistant step is occupied by someone of a different nationality, all silhouetted against the shoeboxes rising up the wall. The lighting overhead is as stark as you get – four unsheathed bulbs, the beams rebounding off the red coal buckets and a wooden currach (a type of small boat) dangling from the ceiling. The bar is at the perfect height for the elbows that echo down its pitch pine planks, the hands that occasionally sweep up the glass for a drink. In two corners, small groups drink together in cosy tongue-and-groove snugs, surrounded by ceramic jars, honeysuckle wine and quirky pictures by the great Jay Killian. Everywhere the banter is in full flow. When the music starts, all ankles tap. If these people are not Irish, they sure want to be.

FACING PAGE: Assorted footwear, raunchy artwork and shelves of shoe boxes line the walls of the former cobbler's workshop.

In a nod to Dingle's cheerful and thriving visitor trade, the pub now boasts its own 'Walk of Fame'.

J. Curran's

An old-fashioned grocery-bar

'I AM AN OLD WOMAN NOW, WITH one foot in the grave and the other on its edge.' For many, these words may send shivers down the spine. They mark the opening paragraph of *Peig*, the astonishingly bleak autobiography of the Co. Kerry *seanachaí* (storyteller) Peig Sayers. For the many generations of secondary school students who were compelled to study *Peig* in Irish, the book represents a low point of their educational career. Remarkable as it is, *Peig* is just not the sort of book one should inflict upon teenagers.

Born in 1873, Peig Sayers was fourteen years old when she went to Dingle to work as a family servant for her father's cousin, James Curran, and his wife, Nell. James had opened a shop-bar on the town's Main Street in 1871. This was where Peig sometimes worked. However, her main role was doing household chores and taking care of the Currans' children as well as James's mother, Nan. Although the work was hard, Peig said she was treated well and felt like a member of the family. At the age of sixteen, ill health obliged her to bid the Currans farewell and return to her family. She later married fisherman

FACING PAGE: *The tongue-and-groove counter and back bar runs down one side of the room, its stools occupied by men and women who know each other well.*

Pádraig Ó Gaoithín and moved to the Great Blasket Island where the majority of her book is set.

When the original James Curran died in 1907, the business passed to his son John, one of the co-founding chairmen of the Irish Volunteers in Dingle. After John's death in 1926, his widow, Mary, ran the shop and bar with her elder son, James. Following James's premature death in 1940, she turned to her younger son, Joe, who gradually took over the business before her death, at the age of ninety-one, in 1966. When Joe died in 1990 it passed to his son James, the present owner.

Like so many of Dingle's fine pubs, Curran's has always doubled as a general merchant. 'They sold everything long ago', says James, pulling out one of the old ledger books. Ledgers such as these provide invaluable archive material for those seeking to track their forebears. In the 19th century, Curran's supplied every business in town; the ledgers are stuffed with billheads from all manner of harness-maker, tailor, newsagent, chemist, baker and clergyman. Trawling through the names, James shakes his head and remarks: 'They're all gone now, every single one of them gone.'

A bacon scale dominates the second counter while, above a snug, shelves are bedecked with milk churns, bronze separators and old stout bottles.

When James says they sold 'everything', he is not far off. The products listed are endless: ropes, twines, seeds, ales, buckets, hams, jams, fishing nets, flowers, lawnmowers and ladies' rubber heels. Drapery was perhaps their greatest business: 'we sold plenty of cloth caps, shirts and boots for the farmers.' The farmers would pile into Dingle on fair days and load their carts with sacks of meal for their animals. The Currans themselves had a small farm outside Dingle; one of the farmyards remains intact to the rear of the pub.

James closes the book and says, 'Potatoes, cabbages, carrots and coal'. As if to emphasize the odd one out, he tells a tale of a farmer who once purchased a sack of flour and a sack of coal. 'He put both sacks on the one cart but it rained heavy on his way home and the coal and flour came together. They decided to make a cake using the black flour anyway. He ate it and when it didn't kill him, they all ate it.'

'There isn't a whole pile of these pubs at all', he says. The temptation to sell must sometimes itch. When David Lean's production team came to Dingle in 1968 to film the controversial epic *Ryan's Daughter*, they tried in vain to buy his Valentia slate floor, offering to replace it with any floor he wanted. In more recent times he has declined a substantial offer that would have seen his pub transported in its entirety to the USA as a 'genuine Irish bar'. That said, he's heard tell of an exact replica of the pub somewhere in America.

In fact, it would be straightforward enough to replicate Curran's. It is a single, square room, a traditional cocktail of tobacco-stained

wallpaper and tongue-and-groove, with snugs in three of the four corners. Shelves stacked with shirts, caps and boots line one wall; James removes them at weekends when the pub tends to become swamped with those looking for a sing-song. Along the walls hang a portrait of his late father, Joe Curran, and images of Dingle in older days – horse races, coursing greyhounds, street scenes – and a chart showing the tariffs for the long-gone local railway back when you could get to Ventry and back for four shillings. The shelf top is lined with a mishmash of oddities, including milk churns, brass spraying machines, binoculars, weighing scales, a manual for Victor lawnmowers and miscellaneous cigarette and whiskey advertisements. 'I put things up there as I gather them', says James. 'Other than that, it's never changed since it opened. And it'll not change with me either.'

Crotty's

KILRUSH – CO. CLARE

One of the cradles of the Irish folk-music revival

Located on the Market Square in Kilrush, the building occupied by Crotty's dates to at least 1832.

FACING PAGE: *The kitchen where the Crottys ate has been left largely as it was, complete with the Vice-Regal stove from Sackville Street (now O'Connell Street) in Dublin. A photo of Mrs Crotty hangs to the right of the fireplace.*

ON 30 OCTOBER 1914, Captain Alexander Vandeleur of the 2nd Life Guards was killed in action on the Western Front. News of his death must have met with mixed reactions back in Kilrush, West Clare. The Vandeleurs had effectively founded the Shannonside town but a hardline eviction policy adopted by Alexander's father during the summer of 1888 had considerably reduced their popularity.

Nonetheless, the death of the thirty-year-old officer must have sent a chill through Miko and Lizzie Crotty. The newlyweds were exactly the same age as the Captain and would likely have known of him from an early age. Indeed, it was only weeks since Miko had obtained a vital document, signed by Alexander's grandfather in 1832, by which he had gained ownership of the pub on the Market Square in Kilrush.

Miko Crotty was born to a farming family from Gower, West Clare, in 1885. When he was seventeen, he took a ship to America where he spent several years working on the railroads. Once he had amassed sufficient money, he crossed the Atlantic once again, arrived at Kilrush and took a lease on the premises that still bears his name today. At the time it was a hardware store but by the time he acquired the premises outright from Bartholomew Culligan on 26 March 1920, Miko had converted it into a pub.

Although Crotty's occupied an enviable position in Kilrush, directly opposite the once thriving market house, it was by no means the only pub in town. Indeed, Kilrush recorded a staggering sixty-eight pubs in a survey of 1921. That was a year in which Ireland's troubles began seriously to worsen. One morning, Miko was apparently taken outside and shot in the leg by an IRA kangaroo court. Quite what he was charged with will probably never be known.

In 1914, Miko married his childhood sweetheart, Elizabeth Markham. Known to music circles as 'Mrs Crotty', Lizzie would go on to become perhaps the greatest concertina player of her age. During their childhood, Lizzie and her sister Maggie had often played together for local house dances, weddings, christenings and

Oliver Reed, Richard Burton, Cyril Cusack and Peter McCarthy are among the many thirsty people to have come through the door.

FACING PAGE: The main bar features original the panel tongue-and-groove ceiling and mosaic tiled walls laid by Italian craftsmen. Bundles of 1950s invoices hang by the window on the wires they were found on. The Dold kit-clock to the left was made before 1914.

'American wakes'. But she was virtually unknown until the RTE broadcaster Ciarán MacMathúna turned up at the pub in the mid-1950s, set up a studio in the kitchen and began recording her at play on her Lachenal concertina. When MacMathúna played such rhythmic tunes as 'The Wind that Shakes the Barley' and 'The Reel with the Beryl' on his radio programme, they were so popular that 'Crotty's of the Square' quickly became a regular haunt for musicians. MacMathúna maintained this esteem was due 'not only to the sweetness of her playing, but also to the sweetness and graciousness of the lady herself'. Long after Mrs Crotty's untimely death from angina in 1960, music was to be heard emanating from the windows of Crotty's both day and night. The pub still hosts traditional music throughout the summer. And, almost half a century after her death, the town of Kilrush hosts a weekend celebration of the life and music of Mrs Crotty every August.

The Crottys were destined to have no grandchildren and, following the death of their daughter Peggy, the pub went up for sale. Fortunately, the couple who purchased it both had strong Kilrush roots. Kevin Clancy's parents ran a pub called The Way Inn in Kilrush. His father Pa had been a school friend of the Crottys' son, Father Tommy. Kevin's wife, Rebecca Brew, also comes from a prominent Kilrush business family. In 1994, Kevin and Rebecca returned from a decade in Europe to take on Crotty's pub. They have also become actively involved in Kilrush's burgeoning cultural scene – Rebecca is one of the co-organizers of Eigse Mrs Crotty and Kevin is one of the coordinators of the Kilrush Musical Society.

Crotty's pub today is effectively a square. In the bottom right is the main bar, featuring a pitch pine counter, a tiny frost-glass snug and a rare plate-glass Smithwick's Ale & Barleywine mirror. This was the room where Oliver Reed, Richard Burton and Cyril Cusack all drank when passing through town. Miko managed to lure an Italian stonemason working on the Catholic church to lay most of the floor, save for the somewhat uneven bar area. An antique Dold kit-clock resounds from behind the bar while bundles of old 1950s invoices hang upon wires in the front window. To the left, a room formerly used to store packages for the national bus company offers intimate seating beneath posters for the once esteemed Kilrush Opera Society. At the back is the Crottys' old kitchen, complete with Vice-Regal stove and shelves of china and crockery, which runs into the old Tap Room at back right. The walls are bedecked in memorabilia relating to the Crotty family as well as posters for the Lisdoonvarna Festivals, The Chieftains at the Sorbonne and various *Fleadh Ceols* (festivals of Irish music).

Crotty's won the prestigious Munster Black and White Pub of the Year in 1998 and was nominated for the 2006 Tourism Bar of the Year. The Clancys have converted the upper floors into a guesthouse and in 2005 they expanded the premises to include O'Dwyer's newsagent next door, with Angela Murphy at the helm of the conversion. The extension has done the pub no harm and Crotty's is arguably the most popular of the twelve pubs that remain open in Kilrush today. Prosperity has arrived in Kilrush at last. The new marina ensures a healthy traffic in tourism and, so long as the nearby power station keeps providing Ireland with a fifth of its electricity, there will always be a strong working population in the locality.

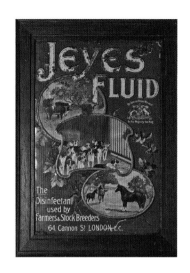

Tigh Neachtain's

GALWAY CITY – CO. GALWAY

Enter a labyrinth of snugs and alcoves in the oldest pub in Galway

FACING PAGE: *Dark corridors lead to intimate snugs of leather seats, timber tables and frosted-glass partitions.*

'BECAUSE, SIR, AN OX CANNOT hold a pistol!' So retorted Richard Martin, MP for Galway, justifying his pioneering defence of animal rights. 'Humanity Dick', as George IV nicknamed him, was one of the most charismatic men in Ireland in the early 19th century. In 1822, he cajoled Westminster into signing into law the first act in the world for animal welfare, from which grew the Royal Society for the Prevention of Cruelty to Animals.

Humanity Dick's association with Galway is today recalled by a modest plaque on the wall of Tigh Neachtain's, the oldest pub in Galway City – and an ISPCA collection box on the bar counter. Jimmy Maguire, the soft-spoken owner, believes his pub formed part of a medieval townhouse built by the Martin family. The Martins originally came to Ireland with the de Burghs in the late 12th century and were one of the celebrated Tribes of Galway. Their heyday arguably began when crusader Oliver Martin found himself sharing a prison cell in Austria with Richard the Lionheart. By the 16th century, the Martins were among the most prosperous families in the west of Ireland, making claims on Connemara for what would ultimately become a colossal estate of 200,000 acres. Indeed, the avenue leading to their headquarters at Ballinahinch Castle was thirty miles long.

'The Martins were very good to their subjects', insists Jimmy, eyebrows rising on the word 'subjects'. 'Particularly during the Famine when their generosity more or less triggered their bankruptcy.' As the power of Ireland's Protestant landlords declined in the 1850s and 1860s, so a new generation of Irish Catholics began to gain a footing in the social hierarchy.

Jimmy's grandfather, Sean Neachtain, was one of four sons born to a poor fisherman from near Spiddal on the shore of Galway Bay. During the 1870s, three of these brothers emigrated to three different continents and all found work in goldmines. One went to South Africa, another to California and Sean himself went to Melbourne which, since the discovery of gold twenty years earlier, had become one of the richest cities in the world. Sean returned to Ireland in 1894 a reasonably wealthy man, and purchased the four-storey building which carries his family name today. Jimmy believes a pub was already in existence here when Sean bought it.

This townhouse was once home to the prosperous Martin family.

The bar boasts one of the best selections of single malts in the west of Ireland. Among the highlights are the Tyrconnell malts, specially bottled for Jimmy by the Cooley Distillery. Galway Hooker Pale Ale is another good seller.

An oriel window overhead certainly dates to the late 18th century. Perhaps it was one of those Galway 'tippling houses' which, as author James Hardiman complained in 1820, were 'most indecorously kept open during the hours of divine worship' so that the 'evening of the sacred day [i.e. the Sabbath] was not infrequently profaned by drunkenness and riot'. The extent to which Sean altered the bar is unknown but much of the interior decoration dates from his short reign.

Sean died prematurely following a heart attack in 1904. His widow, Kate ,was pregnant with what would be their only child, a daughter whom she called Sarah. Kate Neachtain ran the pub until her own death in 1934 when Sarah and her husband, James Maguire, took over. James came from Clonmel and was a descendant of one of the Ulster soldiers who remained in the south after O'Neill and O'Donnell's ill-fated march to Kinsale in 1601 (see p. 46). Sarah ran the pub until the late 1970s when her only son, Jimmy, decided to drop out of college and take on the business. Jimmy was born in the pub and had his childhood bedroom upstairs, clambering up this same staircase when he came back from school with a satchel over his shoulder. 'And here I am', he marvels. 'Still here.'

'Very little has changed', says Jimmy. 'I love old things and the way it was when I got it suited me fine.' In 1992, he extended the premises into an adjoining building, fitting it with 'sanctified' panelling from a convent in Newtown Forbes. A stained-glass door opens into a labyrinth of snugs, alcoves and long rooms, shimmering with pitch pine panelling, leather seats, timber tables and frosted-glass partitions. A further room to the back is walled with maps from Captain G.A. Bedford's extensive survey of Galway Bay in 1847.

Jimmy is passionate about history. He regales his audiences with the tale of Captain Thomas Poppleton, husband to one of the Martins, who became friendly with Napoleon while serving as his gaoler on St Helena. The word is that some decades back, a maid was dusting a mantelpiece at the Poppleton home in Oughterard when she slipped and sent a porcelain snuffbox cracking on the fireplace. Inside was a tiny scroll with a detailed map of St Helena, showing its landing base, garrison strength, gun placements and such like. Surely, says Jimmy, this is concrete evidence that Poppleton was planning to help Napoleon escape. Jimmy sometimes assures his customers that Poppleton took the French Emperor into Neachtain's for a secret pint on his way to St Helena. In fact, he blinks, Christopher Columbus most probably drank a rum here when he called by on his way to the New World.

Towards the end of the 18th century, Humanity Dick founded Galway's first theatre when he built a 100-seater at Kirwan's Lane for his actress wife. The republican patriot Wolfe Tone was one of the leading actors. It is thus fitting that Tigh Neachtain's should have such a keen theatrical bent, much of it stemming from the travelling actors of the Footsbarn Theatre who made the pub their unofficial Connaught headquarters in the 1970s. Posters on the walls bear testimony to the Footsbarn's many performances, as well as Galway's own Druid Lane Theatre and the Irish-speaking Taibhdhearc Theatre. The pub possesses the only complete collection of posters for every Galway Arts Festival since 1978.

Tigh Neachtain's is strong on both literary and musical customers with well-attended traditional sessions a regular feature. It helps, of course, that the pub is located on one of the busiest streets in a city that is alive all year around with a commotion of students, visitors and citizens alike, the atmosphere kept sharp by the music ringing in on the Atlantic breeze. 'Times have changed thankfully', says Jimmy. 'We're all the time busy now. But sure doesn't it take the tedium out of the day?'

Shelves are stacked with old whiskey bottles and boxes for Shaw's soap and Golden Vale cheese.

Thomas Connolly's

SLIGO – CO. SLIGO

Four generations of the same family have kept standards high

ON CHRISTMAS EVE, 1889, CAPTAIN O'SHEA publicly named Charles Stewart Parnell as the lover of his wife, Katharine, and father to three of her children. It was a sombre day for Parnell, the 'Uncrowned King of Ireland', the champion of Irish nationalism for over a decade. The revelation shocked Catholic Ireland to its core and Parnell's Irish Parliamentary Party disintegrated in its wake. By October 1891, Parnell's body lay buried in Glasnevin. Among the millions who mourned his passing was the nationalist Thomas Connolly whose successful campaign to become Mayor of Sligo in 1890 had received a considerable boost when Parnell had attended a civic reception at his pub.

Thomas Connolly made his money on the American railroads in the 1880s and acquired the pub on 16 January 1890. Today, the double-fronted three-storey building looks across the river Garravogue at the shimmering walls of the Glass House Hotel. The area was reclaimed from the river by Sligo merchants in the 1780s. Present owner Gerry Nicholson, a direct descendant of Connolly's sister, believes it was a shebeen of some sort from the outset. The pub was licensed to a Mr Hennigan in 1861, a year after the railway arrived in Sligo. Many early customers had witnessed both the cholera epidemic of 1832 and the famine of 1847, two cataclysmic events that prompted a despondent journalist to declare, 'Sligo is no more'. Sligo somehow bounced back from these horrors and, by Connolly's day, it had become a major brewing and distilling centre, with buoyant rope, linen and leather trades.

Connolly's political career came to an abrupt end with his death from tuberculosis in 1896. His funeral was among the biggest Sligo has hosted. Connolly's daughter became one of the first qualified dentists in Ireland but wretchedly she and her only brother also succumbed to tuberculosis. The riverside pub duly passed to Thomas's bachelor brother, Dennis, a veteran of the

FACING PAGE: *Among the many personal relics of the family is a postcard to Richard Fox from a cousin who emigrated by ship to America in 1934.*

A pot-bellied Romesse stove provides welcome heat to the back of the bar.

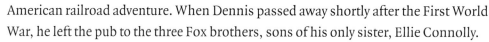

PREVIOUS PAGES: *These three open-sided wooden seating areas, much loved by customers, date to the late 19th century.*

The original grocery box shelves support whiskey jars and bins for Thomas Connolly's famous teas.

American railroad adventure. When Dennis passed away shortly after the First World War, he left the pub to the three Fox brothers, sons of his only sister, Ellie Connolly.

The Fox brothers did much to establish the pub as one of the leading grocery-bars and wine merchants in Sligo. Of particular repute were their teas. Right up until the 1980s, the Donegal bus would stop outside Connolly's so that the passengers could pop in for a cup. The six tea bins from which these famous blends were served are kept beneath a series of wooden arched shelves behind the bar.

The Fox brothers also bottled their own whiskey. 'It would arrive in huge jars and it was up to you to bottle them and decide on the strength', says Gerry. The brass gadgetry involved in this process lines the shelves today, alongside the Avery weighing scales, the Sykes hydrometer, the moisturizer and the original jars. During the 1930s, Sligo was the second biggest port in north-western Ireland. Every week, cargo ships from Poland, Denmark and Scotland would dock, laden with corn, tea, timber and coal. The hardy sailors frequently piled into Connolly's to drink 'rum and blacks' alongside Sligo's indigenous dockers.

Public order within the pub was maintained by Jim Fox, the eldest of the brothers, who had served with the Royal Irish Constabulary from 1882 through until the foundation of the Free State in 1922. The Foxes kept the pub so secure that in 1940 Mayor Mickey Conlon kept his chain of office in the pub's safe.

None of the Fox brothers married. In 1956, following the death of Jim, the last of the brothers, the pub passed to Gerry Nicholson, son of their only sister Katie and her husband, 'Red Tom' Nicholson. In his youth Gerard had won a scholarship to Sligo's Summerhill College, and had been due to embark on a lucrative banking career. However, he turned down the banking option in order to help his uncles run the pub. His wife, Maureen, was a poultry inspector from Kells, Co. Meath, who came to examine chickens in Sligo but instead discovered Gerard, with whom she shared a great passion for horse racing. Gerard died in 1986 and Maureen ran the pub single-handedly until 1992 when her eldest son Gerry came home to take it on.

'It was a crossroads decision', says Gerry. 'Either I stay in the job or I come back here.' Gerry was a Garda

officer with ten years' experience. He served four years in Buncrana, Co. Donegal, and later, after his father's death, operated closer to home in the seaside resort of Bundoran. His time in the force gave him such confidence that he realized he could be his own boss. 'I started here as a kid when it was all about the grocery', he says. 'We've had a great change since then and we're still changing. You can't compete with supermarkets so we closed that side.' Assisted by Frank Conway, the production designer from Jim Sheridan's *The Field*, and Adie O'Donnell, Gerry gave the interior a revamp, shifting snug partitions and counters this way and that in order to create the desired effect.

Sligo is blessed with an above average selection of old-style pubs. Thomas Connolly's is a rare and wonderful premises from its marvellous Kilkenny flagstone floor up. Generous dark tongue-and-groove snugs run along one wall. Timber and glass partitions allow light to flood in while ensuring the spaces remain enclosed and private. Radiators are carefully concealed beneath timber benches. The long bar counter rolls up past the snugs and main bar area, curling towards a pot-bellied Romesse stove at the far end. Miscellaneous pages from the original ledger books, *The Chronicle* and *The Sligo Champion* are framed alongside glass mirrors, tattered calendars and browning photographs. Although he concedes television can be 'a killer' in a pub, Gerry has screens above the bar for sport. He is an enthusiastic athlete himself – his father was Chairman of the Sligo Rovers and a founding member of the Sligo Races in 1955 – and sporting occasions bring important customers flooding into the pub. On such weekends, they go through a barrel of Guinness every hour.

In 1986, Gerry met his wife, Lucia, who runs Nicholson's Pharmacy nearby. 'I sicken them and she cures them', he laughs. Four generations on, Thomas Connolly's continues to be run in a manner of which its founder would surely approve, with the individual drinker still being treated with the respect and courtesy of the old days.

One of several snugs flooded with light reflected from the river Garravogue.

Wall clocks and culinary antiques adorn traditional white-painted pine walls.

The Goulding's Manures clock is one of nearly twenty hanging throughout the pub.

J. & W. Wright's

GLASLOUGH – CO. MONAGHAN

Music, clocks and undertaking come together in this marvellous bar

IN 1858, THE GREAT NORTHERN RAILWAY reached Glaslough, abruptly connecting the small Monaghan village to the main junction at Clones and the wider world beyond. The small estate village boomed as a result. Farmers poured in from far and wide, loading their fattened livestock and harvested crops onto the waiting carriages bound for the big towns of Enniskillen, Armagh, Cavan and Dundalk. The town fair was revived and a cattle market prospered in the centre of the village. It was here, in the late 19th century, that the Patton family built a large limestone coach house.

In the beginning, the intention was simply to provide stabling for horses and security for the carriages. Before long, however, the business had expanded to incorporate a large grain store, a series of coal sheds and a hardware shop; the original winches and green carriage gates remain in place today. By the early 20th century, the Pattons had developed a commercial hotel for travellers, a grocery shop, an oil and petrol station, an undertaking business and a pub.

The Glaslough boom lasted exactly one hundred years. In 1958, the Irish government was obliged to terminate the railway link and suddenly the village was plunged into the backwaters. Always proficient at mathematics, owner David Patton deduced that the Glaslough business was no longer viable. In 1962, he offered the coach house, its hotel and all the affiliated businesses to his manager, Jim Wright. Jim convened with his brother Wallace and before long there was a new sign above the door, 'J. & W. Wright'.

An unusually philosophical visitor information board that stands opposite the pub today declares: 'A village is a living thing and, in order to survive, it must be fed and nurtured. If this happens, the place itself thrives and flourishes, and so in turn do its residents.' Along with the Castle Leslie estate, Wright's has been an integral part of ensuring that, despite the loss of the railway and the grimness of the 1970s and 1980s, Glaslough remains one of the handsomest villages in Ireland.

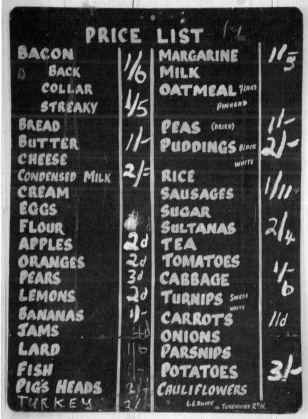

When it operated as a grocery, most of the produce sold at Wright's was grown or made locally.

Heat drifts out across the flagstone floor of the back room. The tongue-and-groove walls are hung with stirrups, a cross-cutter saw, old tack for carthorses and stag antlers.

The Wright brothers continued to run everything except the hotel, which they used as a living quarters. In 1966, Wallace converted the old meal store into what is generally hailed as the first singing lounge in North Monaghan. Glaslough man Joe Corrigan played trombone on the opening night with his band, The Clipper Aces. 'We done everything', he recalls. 'Country and Western, Dixieland jazz, traditional *céili* dances, everything.' Wright's swiftly became a household name for music lovers north and south of the border and business began booming once again.

Wallace Wright died in 1990 and the business passed to his daughter Diane and her husband, Ron Kendrick. The newlyweds had returned to Glaslough the previous year to take over the running of the pub. Although born and raised in Leicester until the age of nine, Ron knew the area well. His mother and father were born locally and the family had moved to Glaslough in the 1970s. Under the Kendricks, the original bar, previously used for storing coffins, was reopened in 1990 as an alternative venue to the 1966 formica lounge bar. The two now operate on a rotating basis depending on the anticipated size of the crowd. *Céilis* continue to be part of the show and birthday parties are frequent, although tighter drink-driving laws have considerably reduced the size of these.

The original bar is known locally as The Olde Bar on account of it not being changed for so many years. Wallace had a passion for clocks and kept them all running in precise beat with Big Ben. As Ron notes with a hint of irony, keeping them constantly wound up requires immense patience. Joe Corrigan recalls coming in here as a child in the late 1940s. The room was filled with farmers drinking tea, eating sandwiches, striking deals and spitting tobacco onto the sawdust-covered flagstone floor. At one end is the old snug where women drank in decades past, now coated in old-style 'Lady Lavery' banknotes. 'They snuck through here,' chuckles Joe, 'closed the door and sat around the fireplace.'

A lovely pine bar painted in a rich, engaging green, stretches beneath a dark tongue-and-groove panelled ceiling, dimly lit by glass globes and hurricane lanterns. Piled up behind the bar are myriad dusty curiosities – his late father's Viking helmet, old china figurines, miniature cars, drums, teapots, a turkey salver, a model of a Conestoga wagon. Heat emanates from a pot-bellied stove at one side. Along the wall hang photographs of Monaghan footballers and local biker groups, a Pears advertisement from 1911 entitled 'Family Worship' and a portrait of Charles Powell Leslie, whose descendants run Castle Leslie.

The Pattons' original bottling room to the back serves as an alternative seating area. Daylight pours through tartan curtains into a room of tobacco-stained walls, furnished with twirly-legged tables and kitchen chairs. Relics of the old days abound on shelves and mantelpieces – the W. G. Edmunds & Co. bottling siphon, a Spong knife sharpener, a cross-cutter saw, old tack for carthorses, a wheel pump, a barometer, a pair of antlers and a sign for 'J. & J. Patton, General Merchants'.

Before insurance costs became too high, Glaslough hosted an annual motorbike rally, which could draw a crowd of anything up to 10,000 people. Ron was himself a keen biker, 'in between the hedges', racking up a personal best at his home race of fifth place on a Yamaha road bike. He was delighted that his pub should be at the hub of it all. Ron's late father, Cecil, was also an enthusiastic biker, frequently powering along the Border roads sporting a Viking helmet made from real hair and cattle horns. He was killed in an accident near Emyvale in 1997. A bench to his memory stands outside the pub. 'Bikes are dangerous things', Ron concedes.

Accepting the inevitable, the Kendricks closed the grocery in 1990, converting the extra space into a family living room. Today their principal business consists of the two bars and the undertaking. 'I was a bit squeamish at first', says Ron of dressing corpses. 'But you get used to it, same as you do taking a picture or driving a car.' Joe Corrigan remembers how in the Wright brothers' day, a funeral cost 'ten bob and ten pence'. That would get you the horse-drawn coach, five dozen bottles of stout, several tins of biscuits and basic groceries for the mourners. 'And the bill would stay sitting on Wallace's desk for so long, it'd be as yellow as a duck's bill.'

Local trombone player Joe Corrigan sits outside Wright's pub, where he first played in 1966.

McConville's
(The Mandeville Arms)

PORTADOWN – CO. ARMAGH

Largely unchanged since 1900, this hotel-bar is steeped in history

ONE HUNDRED AND FIFTY YEARS AGO PORTADOWN effectively belonged to the Montagu family, Viscounts Mandeville and Dukes of Manchester. The family descended from the judge who condemned Sir Walter Raleigh to death in 1618. During the Victorian era, the Dukes made great efforts to improve their landholding in Armagh, planting orchards, developing the cotton industry, building railways and canals, establishing schools and even landscaping a golf course. The family's Irish seat was at nearby Tandragee Castle (today the headquarters of Tayto Crisps).

One of Portadown's main streets was Mandeville Street and at its corner stood The Mandeville Arms, known today as McConville's. A hotel appears to have been situated here since at least 1845. At the time, this part of Portadown was a market shambles, comprising stalls for penning cattle and pigs at the fair days held on the third Saturday of every month. Linen merchants also frequented the area.

The hotel's first proprietor was Ann Edgar, a farmer's daughter from Ballybreagh. Her mother, Mary Bruce, was a descendant of the Scottish king Robert the Bruce and brought the Edgar family a considerable dowry of lands in Co. Down. In 1834, Ann married Henry Hart, a wealthy distiller who later became a lay preacher with the Wesleyan Methodist Church. Ann and Henry Hart lived near Shillington's General Store at 42, Woodhouse Street, Portadown. Their first child, Robert, was destined to become Inspector General of China's Imperial Maritime Custom Service. As Sir Robert Hart, he was one of the central British diplomats in the Orient during the Boxer Rebellion.

The name 'The Mandeville Arms' is still to be found above an old lantern hanging outside the iron-canopied entrance. Higher still stands a decorative folly, with the year '1865' clearly etched for all to see. In that year, as North America was rocked by the assassination of Abraham Lincoln, ownership of the hotel transferred to the McConville family. Rose Anne McConville, heiress to the property, married Paddy McAnallen of the pharmaceutical family. Their great-grandson, Martin McAnallen, sold the pub in 2006 to Andrew Robinson.

The present building is said to date to 1900 and incorporates the original wooden snugs, heavily moulded ceiling and etched-glass windows. Tradition claims some of

A Victorian gas cigarette lighter in the shape of the Tichborne claimant.

FACING PAGE: *Juxtaposed between mirrors, cask tops set into the back bar hold the upturned bottles of spirits and liquor in position, ready to flow.*

TOP: *A portrait of Britain's 'Home Rule' Prime Minister, W. E. Gladstone, by Emilie Chaese hangs over one of the snugs.*

BOTTOM: *Each snug features a match strike and a bell.*

the Russian oak fittings in the bar replicate a design used on the *Titanic*. The original gaslight fittings remain in place, now running on bottled gas. A large mirror promotes 'McConville's Navy Rum', bottled in Portadown and 'made from the finest sugar cane'. The rum was one of several drinks the McConvilles bottled during the early 20th century, including their own McConville's whiskey, Kopke's Invalid Port and some exceedingly strong Australian wine. Andrew has added a useful reserve stock of Old Comber whiskey bottles to this collection, discovered thirty years after the closure of the massive Comber distillery in Co. Down.

Andrew first saw McConville's when he was fifteen and was seized with a desire to one day own the premises. His father, a farmer, had set the concept in motion when he purchased Robinson's Bar on West Street in 1993. Ten years later, Andrew fulfilled his childhood dream when he discovered McConville's was on the market and in danger of being converted into a travel lodge.

McConville's is a listed pub. It is Andrew's intention to extend the property by way of a vaulted corridor through to a new bar, to be called Mary Mac's, incorporating a butcher's shop and off-licence next door. He also plans to renovate the sixteen bedrooms upstairs which, unloved since the 1960s, retain considerable charm, a thin layer of dust running over a complete set of the works of Charles Dickens and an extremely weighty Bible.

One of the bar's features is a gas cigarette lighter in the shape of the man who claimed to be Sir Roger Tichborne, lost heir to a vast estate in Hampshire, whose trial was one of the sensations of the Victorian era. On a shelf above the dimly lit bar, a row of port bottles stand on parade, clad in brown paper bags. Guests either congregate at the bar or in one of the ten intimate leather-seated snugs running through the room. The floor is a particularly wonderful concoction of tiles – cool browns, sky blue, dusty reds – riddled with dusty cracks and fault lines.

Portadown had a rough ride during the final decades of the 20th century, to a large extent due to the Orange Order's annual parade along the predominantly nationalist Garvaghy Road to their church at Drumcree. The Orange Order has always been influential in the town. A hundred metres from McConville's stands a statue of Colonel Edward James Saunderson, a former Grand Master of Belfast, his bronze foot resolutely stamped upon the Home Rule bill, which was such a divisive issue in the lead-up to Irish independence. Over two hundred and fifty officers and men from Portadown died during the First World War but it was arguably the violence of the 1980s and 1990s that caused the town its greatest heartache. In January 1981, a large car bomb exploded outside McConville's, injuring ten people and causing serious damage to shops, offices and flats throughout the area. The building to the left of McConville's was totally destroyed but remarkably the pub lost only its windows and a good deal of the original antique furniture from the bedrooms

upstairs. The surrounding streets were subsequently flattened to make way for a vast shopping complex. Inevitably, the troubles caused property prices in Portadown to tumble.

   'I'm not religious one way or another', says Andrew. 'You can come here whatever age and whoever you are. We have no trouble here. Anything goes. Religion makes no odds.'

Ten intimate wooden snugs run the length of the main bar, each seating four on leather seats.

Kelly's Cellars

BELFAST – CO. ANTRIM

A vaulted emporium of whitewashed walls and tremendous atmosphere

IN THE SPRING OF 1798, a thirty-year-old Belfast Presbyterian came sprinting down a country lane alongside the city's river Farset, dashed through the doors of a nearby tavern and hid himself beneath the counter. For Henry Joy McCracken it was another day on the run. In due course, a detachment of British Redcoats arrived, interrogated the tavern keeper, prodded the grain sacks along the wall and cast suspicious eyes on the silent faces that then watched them leave. McCracken's days were increasingly numbered. On 7 June, the United Irishmen leader commanded a rebel army in open battle with the King's Redcoats outside Antrim. His men were defeated and, five weeks later, McCracken was court-martialled and hanged at Belfast's Cornmarket.

The building was constructed in 1720 as a bonded warehouse for Belfast merchant Hugh Kelly.

The tavern where McCracken hid was Kelly's Cellars, the oldest licensed premises in Belfast and also one of its most alluring. The original two-storey pub was built in 1720 by Belfast merchant Hugh Kelly who kept it as a bonded warehouse; rum, gin and whiskey were his mainstays. It stood in a field just off Crooked Lane, one of the quieter roads leading into Belfast, in an age when the population was little more than 6,000. The river Farset is now underground but, in Hugh Kelly's day, small boats frequently traversed it, laden with flour and wheat.

Belfast has always been a centre of radical politics. In the 18th century, its predominantly Presbyterian population sought to overturn the heavy discriminations they faced under the Penal Laws. Kelly's Cellars became a stonghold for these voices of dissent. It is widely believed that the pub was one of the meeting places for McCracken, Wolfe Tone and the other committee members of the United Irishmen in the run up to the disastrous rebellion of 1798. Over two centuries later, it is easy to imagine such characters plotting revolution here over dark ales and tankards of mead. The pub has changed little since their day.

An unassuming doorway leads into the long, narrow vaulted emporium, a cavern of uneven whitewashed walls, misshapen windows, low arches, splintery whiskey

barrels, gleaming copper pots, crooked enamel signs, rough sandy floors and whispering shadows. Hanging from the old beams above are oil lamps, buckets, brassware, watering cans, kettles, bellows and a dusty harp. The tobacco-stained walls combine tongue-and-groove with the original brickwork and are decorated with memorabilia relating to Belfast's often difficult past. There are portraits of both McCracken and Tone, sepia-toned images of Dublin during the carnage of the Easter Rising of 1916, stark photographs of distraught women gazing at the wreckage of bombs in more recent troubles.

Hugh Kelly, the last of the family to own the pub, died in 1863. Ten years later, the Belfast drinks magnate Sam Young opened the premises. One of the pot-boys working in the pub at this time was 'Wee Joe' Devlin, a charismatic working-class lad who would go on to become the greatest force of nationalism in West Belfast and

Rebel leader Henry Joy McCracken is said to have found safety hiding behind this bar in 1798.

Grandmaster of the Ancient Order of Hibernians. When Devlin helped Sam Young win a seat as Nationalist MP for West Cavan, Young persuaded his charge that he too should enter politics. Devlin's portrait once hung above the bar where he served but has since been superseded by Che Guevara.

On Easter Tuesday, 1941, 180 Luftwaffe bombers struck Belfast in an assault that lasted five-and-a-half hours. Over 900 people died and 35,000 houses were damaged. The back of Kelly's bar was reduced to rubble. The following year, Young, King & Co. sold the pub to visionary businessman Jimmy Tohill. Few believed the near-dilapidated pub stood a chance of surviving. However, the next thirty years were to be a golden age in the history of the bar. Tohill whitewashed the black inner walls and gave the original mahogany wood interior a thorough revamp. He refused to make any structural alterations. 'You shouldn't pull down history', he said. Instead, he decorated the place with odds and ends he had collected – rare coins, chinaware,

copper measures, elephants' teeth, sporting prints and the like. The many
journalists, ship workers, sportsmen, bankers and politicians who drank there
knew it simply as 'The Cellars'. Photographs of some of these still adorn the walls,
such as cross-country champion and sporting journalist Johnny Shanks who used to
hold court from one of these hallowed arches, stubbing out cigarette after cigarette.
Playbills along the walls recall the age when this was a great thespian hang out –
producer Tyrone Guthrie frequently came here looking for props. The novelist Hugh
MacCartan also drank in Kelly's, calling it 'the only authentic Bohemia I have ever
known'. One of the highlights of the Tohill era was a classical mural of Bacchus and
satyrs painted on the ceiling upstairs by a then unknown Sydney Smith. For reasons
difficult to comprehend today, this work was subsequently smothered in red paint.

Belfast is a city that is rapidly discovering a sense of freedom it never imagined
it would have. It is magnificent to see the city centre liberated from barricades and
checkpoints, its streetscapes renovated and modernized, its citizens increasingly
cheerful and debonair. A number of the city centre's pubs still have strict rules
prohibiting patrons from wearing hoodies, tracksuits, tattoos, even caps. You can
only get into some pubs when the landlord unbolts the doors. Kelly's Cellars is
different. Remarkably, the pub was never bombed during over thirty years of
considerable political tension. 'Fáilte Go Teach Ui Cheallaigh' – 'Welcome to the
House of Kelly' – proclaims the welcome above its whitewashed entrance.

Lily and Martin Mulholland purchased the pub in 2004. Like every owner before
them, they have been careful to leave the name above the door and the interior within
just as it was back in McCracken's day. 'The only change is that it's gotten older',
says Mighty Quin, an 88-year-old builder who has been drinking stout in Kelly's for
sixty-six years. Nearly three hundred years after it was founded, Kelly's manages to
find its feet somewhere between everyman drinking pub, political meeting place and
historic museum. Folk music is a regular fare at weekends. As the pints and shorts
slide across the bar, so the session players gather momentum by a roaring turf fire,
a riot of button accordions, banjos, bodhráns, tin whistles, concertinas, flutes and
fiddles. Between the reels, the Irish language is heard throughout the bar, used by
staff and customers alike. There is no television but, if you're hungry by day, you
might get lucky with a bowl of Irish stew, champ and sausages or an Ulster fry.

*Bellows and brass tubs are among the
items hanging from the roof.*

*Kelly's has been a haunt beloved by
judges and lawbreakers for nearly three
hundred years.*

The Crown Liquor Saloon

BELFAST – CO. ANTRIM

The last of the sumptuous Victorian gin palaces

FOR EVERY DARK, MORBID and puritanical Victorian, there was another who adored vivaciousness and light. Belfast is a case in point. The city where they built the *Titanic* was created by citizens with an industrial, rather dour, outlook on life. Its buildings tended to be functional and free of unnecessary décor. There were, nonetheless, certain commercial premises in Victorian Belfast which championed the cause of unadulterated, exuberant flamboyance, and among these was The Crown Liquor Saloon, one of the most fabulous bars in Europe.

Dating to 1826, this landmark establishment originally serviced the six stagecoaches and various jaunting cars passing daily from Belfast to Lisburn. It was renamed The Railway Tavern when the Belfast–Lisburn line opened in 1839. In the 1850s, owner Felix O'Hanlon moved to New York and sold the bar to the Flanagan family. In 1885, Patrick Flanagan returned home after extensive travels in southern Europe with a head full of ideas. A student of architecture, he was greatly impressed by the coffee houses and beer halls of Paris, Vienna and Prague. In time he would use his knowledge of decoration to create the remarkable interior that exists today.

The disestablishment of the Protestant Church of Ireland in 1869 paved the way for a massive boom in church building by the Roman Catholic hierarchy across the country. Skilled artisans flooded in from Europe to complete these jobs. Among the new arrivals were a number of Italian craftsmen who Patrick Flanagan duly cajoled into working on the refurbishment of his family bar. These Italians were responsible for the tiling, glasswork and rich ornamental woodwork that turned Patrick's vision into reality.

This ecclesiastical background explains why, when the sun beams through the decorative windows, this downtown Belfast pub seems more like a Central European baroque church. The impression is further enhanced by the ten elaborately carved

FACING PAGE: *The elaborate marble and tile façade was restored by the National Trust in 2007.*

A long 'altar' bar of Balmoral red granite is divided by columns and faced with merry tiles and a heated foot rest. Look out for the huge casks with their polished brass taps.

PREVIOUS PAGES: Combining rich bordello colours, a scrolled moulded ceiling, elaborately carved screens and ornate wooden snugs, The Crown is one of the most fabulous pub interiors in Europe.

wooden snugs, lettered A to J, and by no means dissimilar to confessionals. These snugs – or 'boxes' to use the colloquial – feature black upholstered seats, nickel plates for striking matches, and an antique push-bell system, common in Victorian times, to alert staff to one's needs. Guarding the entrance to each snug is a heraldic lion or gryphon, their wings and talons now carefully repaired.

The Crown combines a delightfully ostentatious décor with a down-to-earth and mellow ambience. The embossed ceiling boasts a splendid combination of primrose yellow arabesques, rich ruby reds and seductive gold rosettes. The mosaic floor is a mixture of black and white chequers and a terracotta and blue chevron design straight from *The Arabian Nights*. The brocaded walls and wooden columns are decorated with highly patterned tiles, feathered motifs, carvings and mirrors. Painted glass curls in every direction, a vivid medley of amber, crimson and green shells, fairies, pineapples, fleurs-de-lis and clowns. These colourful decorative windows fronting the bar were originally intended to shield customers from inquisitive passers-by.

The Crown is one of the last of the great Victorian 'gin palaces' that once flourished in the industrial cities of Britain. In 1947, Carol Reed copied the ornate

interior for the set of his award-winning film noir, *Odd Man Out*, with James Mason
starring as a fatally wounded IRA man taking refuge in one of the snugs. In 1978,
Sir John Betjeman, the Poet Laureate, virtually insisted the National Trust acquire
this 'many-coloured cavern'. Between 1970 and 1976, twenty-eight bombs exploded
in the Europa Hotel across the road. Not surprisingly, the collateral damage was
considerable, even if the bar stools continued to be defiantly occupied by the same
neutrally minded drinkers who had always frequented the pub. In 1981, the Trust
carried out a sympathetic restoration, restoring the bar to its full Victorian glory.

When the smoking ban was introduced to Northern Ireland's pubs in 2007,
the National Trust sent in a team of fifteen specialists to give the bar a thorough
clean up. Somehow they managed to keep the pub open throughout while, as far as
practicable, they scrubbed and restored every aspect of plastering, woodwork, tiling
and glass. This latest restoration has ensured that, against all the odds, Patrick
Flanagan's remarkable creation has emerged from the Troubles looking better
than ever.

*Ten elaborately carved wooden snugs
run the length of The Crown, capped by
heraldic lions and gryphons.*

House of McDonnell

BALLYCASTLE – CO. ANTRIM

This pub has remained in the hands of the same family since 1766

FACING PAGE: *Bentwood chairs and a cast-iron Edwardian table stand on a tiled floor laid in the 1960s.*

The pub has been in the same family for an astonishing fourteen generations.

'I WAS BORN UPSTAIRS WHEN MY AUNT Mary owned the pub', says Tom O'Neill. 'In those days the midwife got about on a bicycle so they thought it better I be born here on the street than have her cycle way out – uphill all the way – to my father's farm.' Forty years later, when his aunt Mary McDonnell died without children, it was Tom who inherited the pub. He was the eldest son of Mary's only sister, Helen. The new heir considered the name emblazoned on the broken glass above the door. It had been 'The Store' for a hundred years. Tom decided to rename it 'The House of McDonnell'. 'I'm an O'Neill,' he explains, 'but my mother was McDonnell and the pub has been McDonnell for fourteen generations.'

Castle Street, upon which the pub is located, was effectively an avenue for a castle, since demolished, erected in 1609 by the first Earl of Antrim. The earliest licence for the pub dates to 1750, shortly before it was leased to a Mr M'Gildowney. By the time Archibald McDonnell took over the lease in 1766, Ballycastle was enjoying a golden age of prosperity. The boom was spearheaded by an entrepreneurial gentleman, Colonel Hugh Boyd, under whose leadership the coastal town became home to a glassworks, several salt and soap factories, at least two breweries, ten tanning yards, extensive quay and docking facilities and a major export trade in Antrim coal. Colonel Boyd died in 1765 and the local economy went into a slump. The harbour slowly filled with sand and the grandiose quay was washed away by stormy seas. During the 19th century, Ballycastle rediscovered itself as a seaside resort, boosted by the arrival of the railways and the erection of a new pier. Today, the town enjoys the dual benefits of being both a busy seaside resort and an 'all year round' market town, with a fair every month and a market every Tuesday.

In 1898, 'The Store' passed to Tom's grandfather, Randal McDonnell, a big, broad-shouldered man few dared mess with. Tom points at a mirror for McAllister Irish Whisky and recalls a time when the Ballymena distiller James McAllister fell out with his grandfather. 'Randal clobbered him and put him in a barrel in the back yard.' The origin of the quarrel is unknown but 'no supplies were brought from McAllister between 1914 and 1928'. In the 18th century, Archibald McDonnell had run the pub as a spirit-grocery, with stabling for horses and coaches to the back. His descendant

92

A large mirror from the now disbanded Coleraine distillery delineates the end of the main bar and the entrance to the warm fire of the backroom.

Randal ran it as a spirit-grocery bar of the type more commonly found in the south of Ireland. In 1921, Randal closed the grocery section and installed a pitch pine bar the length of the room. To maintain a sense of intimacy, he inserted an oak and frosted-glass partition half-way down. As Tom notes, the partition was an unintentionally symbolic move as 1921 was the same year the six counties of Ulster (Antrim included) were partitioned from the rest of Ireland. The original Victorian interior was otherwise left intact.

When Randal died in 1931, the pub passed to his eldest daughter, Mary, a spinster. For the next four decades, Mary ran the pub in the unobtrusive, pious and proud manner one would expect of a Ballycastle landlady. Tom indicates a dozen African hardwood bar stools he commissioned from a specialist joiner in Co. Down. 'My aunt didn't approve of bar stools', he says. 'She reckoned it meant people would sit around too long.' Customers seated on these African stools today have the added quirk of being able to rest their feet on a brass rail salvaged from HMS *Drake*, a British war cruiser torpedoed off Rathlin Island in 1917. Elsewhere, bentwood chairs and three-legged stools are scattered around. 'Those old flagstone floors were never level but three legs gets you steady', explains Tom.

Most of what one sees in the House of McDonnell is old world from the classic black light switches and coat hooks beneath the counter to the keyhole clock that gongs above the bar. This was an old man's pub and to a large extent it still is. 'We don't do refurbishment', says Tom. The only change he has made was to strip the walls of their heavily embossed anaglypta paper. 'It was on so thick, we nearly had to use a shovel.' In its place, he put a wallpaper 'almost identical' to the William Morris pattern that was there in 1910. Decades of cigarette smoke has given the entire room a sepia hue from the nicotine-stained photographs along the beams to an equine statuette above the bar called 'The White Horse'. 'The tobacco's turned him bay', laughs Tom. The room is lit by a variety of lamps – swan-neck, converted gas, old seamen's lamps. Some of the daylight that comes through the window is filtered through overlaid strips of red Bristol glass, providing the slightest hint of a Bavarian ambience.

The back of the bar is a bottled miscellany broken by distillers' mirrors – a pair of gold and silver embossed Wilsons, an Old Bushmills, a massive frame from

Coleraine, another from the unfortunate McAllister. Advertisements for Cantrell & Cochrane's ginger ale and D'Arcy's stout are found alongside prints of the St Albans Grand Steeple Chase of 1832. A rare flash of the contemporary is found in a wooden fiddler carved by local sculptor and chainsaw maverick Frank Browne.

Tom sits down on a bench in a small snug just off the main bar and runs his fingers over a series of rare Bass ashtrays set into the wall. 'I remember when I was a wee man, there was a cast-iron stove in here and a pipe running through the wall. It was just somewhere to boil a kettle or to sit beside if it was cold.' His great-great-grandfather, David O'Neill, was a ferryman, escorting both people and cargo over the turbulent waters between Antrim and the Scottish coast. One of his sons purchased the farm outside Ballycastle where Tom now lives with his wife. 'We're right on the coast here', says Tom. 'And there's not too many customers out at sea.' Nonetheless, he is content with the crowd of regulars he gets. Every Friday night, the House hosts music, from Flamenco guitars and Breton drums to the simple, uncluttered traditional music of north-east Antrim. Tom is in no hurry to chase the crowds that flock to the coast in the summer. 'Now that times have got more settled, we get a lot more visitors from the south and I do like that.' Above his head are the arms and crest of the McDonnell family who have now run this same establishment for 240 years. Their motto is 'Toujours Pret' (Always Ready) and it is Tom's aim to be just that.

Antique Bass ashtrays from Newhalls are inset into the snug wall.

Classic black Bakelite switches maintain the timeless ambience.

Rural Charm

Plain in décor, fundamental in purpose, the Irish country pub is a symbol of the rapidly vanishing world of old Ireland – men clad in peaked caps and overcoats, perched on mismatched bar stools, sipping stout and strong whiskey. Yet while many have closed in recent years, many other rural pubs struggle on, run by the same families who ran them a hundred years ago and who are determined to keep up the old ways. And Ireland's debt to these pubs is great, for it was from such places that Irish music was brought back from the brink of extinction to its present-day popularity.

Gartlan's, Kingscourt, Co. Cavan.

O'Connell's

Farmers stomp on the stone floor and warm their hands by the coal fire

The stout black pub features in the Guinness brewery's annual Christmas television advertisement.

IN ANCIENT TIMES THERE EXISTED in Ireland a people called the Fianna, a band of semi-independent warriors who lived in the forests. In times of war, the kings of Ireland regularly sought their expertise. Their golden age came to an end during a mighty battle fought in the Gabhra valley of Royal Meath in the early 5th century AD. Their commander, Oscar, grandson of Fionn MacCool, and his enemy, High King Cairpre Lifechair, killed one another during the fight. When Cairpre's beautiful daughter Achall heard of her father's death, she instantly 'died of grief'; her body was laid to rest in a mound on top of a nearby hill.

Many centuries later, St Columba, the man who introduced Christianity to the Picts of Scotland, founded a monastery on this same hill where Achall was buried. When Vikings later ransacked his island retreat at Iona, Columba's followers returned to the hilltop monastery where they briefly hid a shrine containing their beloved saint's relics. They called the hill 'Skryne', meaning 'shrine'. Today, the two most notable buildings at Skryne are a weather-beaten 14th-century church and a public house founded by one James O'Connell in the 1870s and inherited by another James O'Connell in the 1930s.

Born in New York, the latter James was a teenager when his family returned home to run their grocery bar in Ireland. His mother cried for a year after they returned, says Mary O'Connell, the present landlady, known far and wide as 'Mrs O'. James was destined for the priesthood but, during the Troubles, he abandoned the seminary at Maynooth and signed up with Eamon de Valera's Irregulars on the eve of the Irish Civil War of 1922. In time he met Mary Clynch from Dunsany and took her as his wife. His widow now keeps his photograph, resplendent in his uniform, close at hand.

'We had a huge family', laughs Mrs O. 'A boy and a girl. Well, for me it was huge. But Glory be to God, I had no brothers or sisters and I didn't know what hit me when I got married and settled here.' By then, the grocery was the main business. 'We had two cows for milk but everything else we got in.' A pony and trap from Shackleton's would make its way up the bumpy path, laden with flour, wheaten meal for brown bread, flake meal for porridge and bran mash for sick horses and suckling mothers. Rashers, sausages and ham came all the way from McCarron's butchers in

Monaghan. James rarely had a moment's breath, save for his annual pilgrimage to the Galway Festival. 'I remember him out in the yard, all the time, working through the frost and snow.' One of his weekly missions was to go to the train station at Drumree to collect fresh kegs of Guinness.

Exuding the ambience of a living room, a mantelpiece is bedecked with Dutch clogs, floral teapots and dried flowers.

O'Connell's is essentially a cinnamon-hued step back in time to a 1950s country bar. 'We have a certain standard of living even though we have no carpets', explains Mrs O. 'If it doesn't suit you, then go on and don't come back.' The grocery is virtually no more, but you can still see the shelves where everything was stacked, row upon row of chocolates, sugar and pineapple slices. Farmers, well known to one another, congregate beneath the tongue-and-groove ceiling, stomping their feet on the rough stone floor, warming their hands by the coal fire. Windows are framed by wooden panel shutters. This was the room where Neil Jordan filmed the pub scenes for *The Last September*, his adaptation of Elizabeth Bowen's novel. Beneath a Walsh & Sons wall clock hang pictures of the county's victorious football teams; the local club has had at least one player on all seven of the Meath teams that have won the All-Ireland. Rudyard Kipling's 'If' unfurls alongside extracts of local history, imaginatively designed banknotes from times past, pictures of Ireland's Triple Crown champions, and the letters of locals expressing concern about the new motorways steaming across the once mystical landscape, hurtling across gentle streams and bulldozing hidden ringforts where dead warriors rest.

The pub is well known to the equine community, with the Ward Union, the Tara Harriers and Goldburn Beagles pausing for seasonal refreshments, and the race-going crowds calling by on their way back from Navan and nearby Fairyhouse.

With its mismatched chairs, mauve carpet and tartan curtains, the back room brings to mind a 1950s tea-room. The piano on the back wall has lived through many a memorable night.

FACING PAGE: Rickety stools, simple partitions and overhead strip lighting fill O'Connell's with the charm of old Ireland.

Mrs O has never taken a drink in her life. 'My husband said I was bad enough without the drink', she says with a merry chuckle. She adores talking, discussing the news of the day, encouraging creativity and intelligent banter from her customers. She's eager to establish connections, to prove that in Ireland there are only two degrees of separation. She rarely leaves the building, save for Mass. She feels so strongly that men should be at home with their families on Sunday afternoons that she continues to close the pub for the so-called Holy Hour.

Mrs O, a native Irish speaker, has lately entertained two coaches of bewildered Japanese tourists who arrived unexpectedly, waving beer vouchers and tin whistles, with 'genuine Irish pub' written on their itinerary. Mrs O knows times are changing fast. To wander just beyond the pub and stand in the grounds of the ruined abbey, letting the wind rush through your hair and beholding the sumptuous views, one feels a sense of extraordinary antiquity. Humans have stood on this spot for a long time, even since before poor Achall's day. But only a handful of generations will ever have the privilege of enjoying sundowners at Mrs O's.

E. Butterfield's
(The Harp Bar)

BALLITORE – CO. KILDARE

A rare pub that has been run by three female generations of the same family

Dating to the late 18th century, the two-storey public house bore witness to the violence of the 1798 rebellion.

RIGHT: *Few symbols are more evocative of Ireland's struggle for independence than a golden harp set upon a green ground. Here, the harp is portrayed as the romantic goddess Erin.*

FACING PAGE: *Philomena Creagh and her brother, Jim Butterfield, were two of twelve children raised in a house close to the pub.*

WHEN THE WIND BLOWS, ITS BREEZE tickles every string of a harp evenly. For Wolfe Tone and his fellow United Irishmen, in pursuit of a symbol to encapsulate their fundamental belief that all men be treated as equals, irrespective of faith, such an inherently Irish instrument was perfect. When the rebels gathered across Ireland in 1798, it was the golden harp on the green flag that flew highest of all.

It is a curious irony that the village of Ballitore in Co. Kildare should be home to a pub known as The Harp. In 1798, the peaceful Quaker community who lived here witnessed an appalling episode of bloodshed when the doctor and other elders were dragged from their homes and slaughtered on the street. It is difficult to imagine such events when strolling through the sleepy village some two hundred years later. Nonetheless, the consequences of that tumultuous summer still drift through the air, carried on the uilleann pipes and impassioned baritones that gather in The Harp to sing of a Wednesday evening.

The Harp Bar has always had that name but it has been called other things too. One hundred years ago it was owned by John Horan, a bachelor who lived above the grocery-bar with his two spinster sisters. Since 1936, the name above the door has been that of 'E. Butterfield'. 'E' stands for Elizabeth Butterfield, née Nolan of Kildoon, grandmother of Lisa Creagh who runs the pub today. Indeed, it was Lisa's mother, Philomena, who operated the pub during the last three decades of the 20th century, making it one of those rare pubs to have been run by three female generations of the same family in direct succession. Philomena was the youngest of the twelve Butterfield children, all raised in a large house near the pub. All the

siblings left Ballitore save Philomena and two brothers, Gerry and Jim, both butcher-farmers.

Dating to 1780, the pub is a straight-forward one-room affair, with flagstone floors, rustic whitewashed walls and rough-hewn farmyard doors and arches with the wood peeling off. The bar is a solid piece of

102

The original box-drawers, once stocked with herbs, spices, snuff and plug tobacco, billow behind an old rough-hewn bar. In arched cavities above are a harp, a railway lantern, a Brownie camera and an advertisement for Bendigo Plug Tobacco.

timber set upon a wall of old planks, reminiscent of some weather-beaten pirate ship. The shelves behind carry miscellaneous oddities – a harp, a hunting horn, an advertisement for Bendigo Plug Tobacco, a railway lantern, a Brownie camera. To the right are ten old grocery drawers, recalling a not-so-distant time when the pub operated as the village store. Customers sit in close proximity, on stools, chairs and old church benches. The endangered art of communal banter is encouraged with Lisa behind the bar, her laugh as merry as wedding bells. Red embers glow from a vast brick fireplace, enchanting the words that whistle to and fro. Lisa's mother removed the snug partitions where women of another age used to enjoy a secretive hit of snuff tobacco along with a glass of stout. The left-side snug is now home to a pedal organ created by John Malcolm & Co., which takes centre stage on musical evenings.

It is impossible to live in Ballitore and not be engrossed by history. The village's star pupil was Edmund Burke, one of the greatest philosophers and political thinkers of the Georgian period. His tutor, Abraham Shackleton, was the ancestor of another local hero, the polar explorer Ernest Shackleton, who grew up just outside the village. Local farmers still talk of the Wizard Earl of Kildare whose ghost gallops around the nearby ring-fort of Mullaghmast, while more ghosts emerge from the mists in the form of forty local chieftains treacherously massacred at this same ring-fort in 1577. Indeed, Lisa's grandmother was old enough to know some of the 800,000 people who attended Daniel O'Connell's famous Monster Meeting at Mullaghmast in 1843.

Like any pub, Butterfield's has photographs of great moments from times past, including a splendid black and white one of six men, all wearing cloth caps, seated at the bar in 1963.

'And they're all dead?' I ask.

'They're not all dead!', hollers a cloth-capped old man at the corner of the bar and everyone laughs. Dan Mackey has been a patron of Butterfield's for as far back as anyone can recall. He was a farm labourer all his life, working in an age when there was 'nothing, only a spade and fork and no hydraulics at all'. He enjoyed the farming life. 'When you got home, you hadn't a care only that you could get something to eat. You're better off than the people now with their mortgages and two cars. Unless you had nothing to eat!' Dan is of the view that life goes full circle. 'The farmer will be back', he says. 'You might call me mad but I'm telling you now, the wheel will keep turning and the horse and cart will be back.' Whether Dan's forecast comes good or not, it is hoped that the bloodline of Elizabeth Butterfield will still be running the pub a hundred years from now.

A vast open-hearth brick fireplace smokes beside an organ, marking the space where musicians gather on Wednesday evenings. Old tables and chairs are scattered randomly across a cracked flagstone floor.

M. J. Byrne

In the 17th century this was almost certainly a shebeen for mountain travellers

'THERE WAS NO SUCH THING AS STABBING or kicking at that time. If you pulled a knife or kicked a man when he was down, the rest of the lads would turn on you. But the boys would always shake hands after half an hour and have a drink together.' That's the way both Pa Byrne and his friend George Thomas remember fights in Greenane in the good old days. And there were plenty of fights between the rival families who lived up in the glen beyond. In the winter of 1580, an army of 3,000 English soldiers came clattering into the Glenmalure Valley in an attempt to subdue the mountain men. Under the leadership of Fiach MacHugh O'Byrne, the Wicklow

Large bottles of Guinness, served at room temperature, are part of the staple diet for many a Wicklow mountain man.

warriors came howling from the woods with sufficiently sharp swords, spears and axes to leave over eight hundred Englishmen dead by the close of day. It was the greatest defeat the English had yet experienced in Ireland. Fiach was killed in action seventeen years later and his pickled head sent to London.

Pa Byrne is not sure if he's related to Fiach MacHugh. He concedes there may be more to it than coincidence that the family-owned pub he inherited a quarter of a century ago is situated an axe's throw from the ancient O'Byrne stronghold of Ballinacor. The name 'M. J. Byrne' above the door refers to his mother's father, doubling up the Byrne patronymic. Pa's father farmed the land nearby and married M. J.'s daughter during the latter months of the Irish War of Independence. Pa, the second youngest of nine, was born in 1930 and lives in a house next to the pub with two of his sisters and his dog Sandy.

'If there's any bit of sun at all, we get it here', says Pa. Sure enough, Greenane (Grianan in Irish) translates as 'a summer residence'. Despite such positive credentials, the hamlet has somewhat declined over the past two decades. In Pa's youth there were two pubs, a bakery, a wheelwright,

a post office and a chapel. All have been abandoned or converted to private residences so that today the only commercial properties that remain are Pa's pub and the Greenane Farm Museum.

Pa Byrne, pictured here with his dog Sandy, inherited the pub from his mother's family in the 1980s.

The building probably dates to the 17th century and was almost certainly a shebeen for travellers crossing the mountain pass between Aughrim and Dublin. The original thatch roof was galvanized in Victorian times, then slated in the 1930s. Wooden boxes once full of spices and tobacco recall its heyday as a grocery-bar. After the village baker closed down, a bread van came on a daily trek from Donnelly's of Rathdrum. George Thomas, who lives in an isolated farmhouse two miles away, remembers the same van driver leaving a daily loaf in his gateway. The counter over which such bread transactions took place is still there. However, the pub benefited from an old-fashioned revamp when Greenane Bridge was selected by director Neil Jordan for one of the scenes in his Oscar-nominated biopic *Michael Collins*.

Pa still draws a good crowd for funerals and at weekends, particularly when local musicians come and settle in for the night. Inevitably business has declined considerably for roadside establishments like his since the drink-driving laws came in. Perhaps his greatest commercial loss has been the customers who came in daily to drink anything up to fourteen pints in a row. 'They'd all be singing in the end.'

The decoration in M. J. Byrne's is minimal and untouched. A fluorescent light overhead rebounds off a tiled floor, laid down over the original slabs in the 1950s. A pot-bellied Romesse stove steams gently between tables. Behind the bar rests a

Tattered chairs and sofas gather around kitchen tables and a Romesse stove.

safe that someone once tried to elope with in a wheelbarrow. 'We know who was behind it but we won't name any names, God rest him', says George. The walls behind the bar are lined with shooting trophies won by Pa when he was a marksman with the FCA (*An Fosa Cosanta Aitiuil*, Ireland's volunteer army reserve) during the 1950s. 'Shooting rabbits as a young fellow stood me in good stead', he suggests.

George drank in M. J. Byrne's for many decades. However, since the pub closed its grocery section he has been obliged to visit the supermarket in the nearby town of Rathdrum. As a result, when he arrived at the pub, Pa said, 'Hello George, I haven't seen you for a long time'. George ordered a bottle of Guinness and the two men began to reminiscence about characters who drank here in times past. Among these was a quiet old war veteran who had lived many years in Australia. 'If he liked you,' says Pa, 'he'd tell you of the things he saw.'

Happier memories concern the annual 'Klondyke Gold Rush', as it was known, when carts, wagons and horses came cantering into Greenane from all directions on the last Sunday in July. The catalyst for this mayhem was the hunt for the fraughans (wild bilberry) in the surrounding hills. Asses and jennets would be hastily tied to the bars along the windows of M. J. Byrne as the hunters bolted into the hills. Traditionally the berries picked by the young men would be baked into a tart by their sweethearts, which would be served up at the 'Fraughan Sunday' dance that evening. But if you didn't have a sweetheart, recalled Pa, 'there was a fantastic price for them in England'.

Local bachelor George Thomas lives a contented old-world existence in a one-storey farmhouse nearby, without electricity.

P. F. Smyth

The best advice the barman ever got was to stay playing the piano

The original grocery shelves in this room dating to 1821 are painted in a rich lacquered red. The wainscoting was installed by Michael's friend Ned Byrne.

NEWTOWN IS A VILLAGE WITH ONE PUB, one school, one church and not a lot else. The church is one of the finest barn-type gothic churches in Ireland with a spectacular ceiling attributed to an Italian craftsman on the run from the law. Although it opens daily, the church's big day is, of course, Sunday. That's when Michael Smyth cranks up the organ and lets his knuckles ripple. For some in the flock, Michael's distinctive style may still be echoing though their head from the night before. When not playing in St Patrick's, Michael is the proprietor and piano player of P. F. Smyth, one of the last old-style cabaret bars in the country.

P. F. Smyth is also one of Ireland's oldest licensed premises run by the same family, with records going back to the mid-1740s. The Smyth family descend from an English Protestant who settled locally in the mid-17th century. The present bar was built in 1821, during the watch of Robert Smyth, and incorporates the walls of a 16th-century cottage. Robert's son Patrick Francis Smyth was born in the 1820s and operated as an auctioneer from the premises. Astonishingly,

FACING PAGE: *Pin-striped wallpaper and red leather sofas ramble across a Navan carpet exuding classic club elegance.*

At its peak, Smyth's of Newtown was probably the greatest session bar in Co. Carlow. The décor was inspired by the owners' travels in the Mediterranean and America.

P. F. Smyth, for whom the pub is named, was Michael's grandfather. How many people living today have grandfathers who were on first name terms with veterans of the Napoleonic Wars?

Michael Smyth was born above the pub in 1926 and has lived here all his life. His likes include travel, the colour red and anything melodic from rousing Schumann to Percy French. He learned piano at the Leinster School of Music in Dublin but it was his parents who instilled his passion. His father, Joseph, was a fine tenor and, while managing Kennedy's pub on Dublin's Capel Street during the 1890s, sang for such literary greats as Bram Stoker and Sean O'Casey. Michael's mother, Annie, was an accomplished violinist. An aunt taught piano in Paris; an uncle was the organist in Bagenalstown. But the love of music extended beyond the Smyth family, and Michael remembers how in his childhood every farmhouse in the parish possessed a much-treasured piano. As a teenager, Michael played piano in the bar but, being the barman, had to stop every time anyone wanted a drink. 'And then this very old man said to me one time "you get somebody to serve the drink and you stay playing the piano".' It was arguably the best advice Michael ever received.

In time, Michael and his elder brother Patrick, established 'Smyth's of Newtown' as the premier music hall in Co. Carlow. By the late 1960s, they could no longer cope with the crowd. They extended westwards, creating a new piano lounge with the sort of ambience you'd expect of a Roaring Twenties cruise ship. A flamboyant mixture of Art Deco and the Drones Club, distilled with a keen Carlovian eye, this vast room seats 350 and, 'if you didn't come before nine on a Saturday night, you had to stand'. At its peak, six girls ran about taking orders and clearing the debris while the crowd swayed to the tunes coming from the grand piano. Although well off the beaten track, half a dozen distinctive signposts pointed the way from every adjoining county.

P. F. Smyth's jubilant reign came to an end with the toughening of Ireland's drink-driving laws. The huntsmen who gathered in the days of the Kellistown point-to-point dared not stay long. The farmers who frequented during quiet times also vanished. Although Saturday nights still draw a lively crowd, Michael believes the days of the country pub are numbered. 'Paying rates, electricity,

The piano lounge was built in the 1960s in response to the pub's increasing popularity.

heating, public liability insurance . . . it just doesn't add up', he says. 'It's a tremendous pity because the people who come here are very civilized. None of them are ever drunk and that's a fact. It was a great help to people who lived down lanes and in farms that they could come out here and talk and hear the news.'

Smyth's busiest moments now come when mourners assemble for tea and sandwiches after a funeral in St Patrick's church. Michael plays the organ at such services, as he has for thirty-five years – which is why the Pope recently sent him a medal and a certificate. One such funeral was for his wise, gentle elder brother Patrick, who died suddenly in 2004. Today, Michael runs the pub with his younger brother Robert, who for many years was a teacher, first in Algeria, then in Paris.

There's something epic and ghostly about the piano lounge today, with its empty sofas, silent tables and stoic pillars. 'We had a great time down through the years', says Michael, bending his knees at the magnificent grand piano he imported from Hamburg in 1972. 'The piano's lasted well,' he muses, unlocking the keyboard, 'and it's had a hell of a lot of playing.' His 81-year-old fingertips fall upon the ivory keys and a lilting saloon-bar number echoes out across the floor. The tune is called 'Hard Times Come Again No More' by Stephen Foster.

M. O'Shea

A candy-striped bar and stacked hardware give this bar a unique charm

Michael O'Shea ran the premises as a grocery, select bar and hardware store until his death in 1985. Today, it is run by his grandchildren.

BACK IN THE GOOD OLD DAYS WHEN kings were powerful people, Dermot MacMurrough, King of Leinster, took a trot around his kingdom in pursuit of a suitable place to build castles. One of his chosen sites was Borris, a gentle hill at the foot of Mount Leinster, near the banks of the river Barrow. In 1731, Dermot's descendant Morgan Kavanagh built the rambling Borris House where the Kavanagh family still resides today. It is by no means an easy business maintaining an estate as old as Borris. For the incumbent heir, inheriting a big house can, to paraphrase novelist Elizabeth Bowen, land one somewhere between a predicament and a *raison d'être*. The temptation to sell the lot and move to the Caribbean is overruled by the spirit of all those previous generations who have somehow managed to hold the fort.

Precisely the same conundrum faces the O'Shea family who own and run one of the village bars across the road from the stone walls of the Borris demesne.

FACING PAGE: Pastes, glues and twines are shelved above a passageway through to the Tap Room where musicians play.

The main bar area is painted in traditional brightly coloured candy-stripes.

The building has been operational as a grocer-bar since the 19th century. In 1934, a tough-talking farmer's son from nearby St Mulllins purchased the premises and erected a new sign over the door: 'M. O'Shea – Select Bar'. Known as the 'Bossman', Michael O'Shea had served his time as an apprentice barman in Ferns and nearby Graiguenamanagh during the 1920s and decided the work suited him. In fact, a lot of work suited him: tea, wine, spirit and provision merchant, family grocer, hardware, timber, coal, iron, wool and corn store trader, Cushendale Blankets agent, the Bossman did the lot. His ledgers are held above the bar today, each transaction precisely recorded, a peculiar chronicle of who bought tomatoes, bread and coal, and how much they paid. Most of the goods were kept in a hardware store next door while more commonly sought supplies were displayed behind the bar.

The Bossman's wife, Anastasia, had a custom of giving away free bread and milk to the poor hill people when they came down from Mount Leinster. It wasn't a tradition the Bossman warmed to. 'Grandad wouldn't let her work in the bar because she'd always give away stuff', recalls their granddaughter, Olivia O'Shea. 'She'd have a full kitchen every time you went in, serving them all food and not charging any of them.'

Anastasia died in 1982 and Michael followed three years later. Their son Jim and his wife, Carmel, duly took over. It was during this era that the pub became the establishment of choice for Denny Cordell, trainer of horses, greyhounds and, above all, rock legends. In cahoots with Island Records founder Chris Blackwell, Denny produced records for acts such as Procol Harum, Joe Cocker and The Cranberries. After Denny's unexpected death in 1995, his wake was held in O'Shea's. 'They played every version of "Danny Boy" there ever was', recalls Olivia. The nearby Gowran Park racecourse hosts a day in his honour every September. Year after year, the craggy-faced rockers who knew Denny make their pilgrimage to O'Shea's to commemorate the music man.

The rough-topped, candy-striped bar begins virtually at the entrance and runs in an L-shape around the inner wall. Directly overhead hang a miscellany of classic hardware goods, including luggage straps, sieves, oven gloves and a Wellington boot. Brass piping meanders along the overhead ceiling, seemingly held in place by thick black-painted wrought-iron pillars. To the right, behind an old weighing machine, stands a wall of shelves holding carpenter's wares – masonry nails, breeze-block nails, staples, split-links and chipboard screws for every hole and socket. Shelves are stocked with batteries, light bulbs and other compelling items that might suddenly catch one's eye while pontificating over a creamy pint.

'Its quieter at the minute but so is everywhere', says Olivia who now runs the business with her brother Michael. 'We used to have a lot of people who'd come in for three or four pints and go home. But with the drink-driving laws, they don't come anymore.' Olivia believes the challenges ahead will be many but, with tradition in their blood, the third generation of O'Shea publicans will somehow hold the fort.

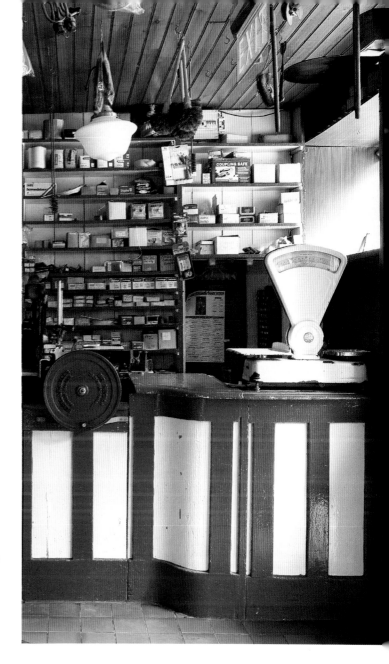

An old weighing machine marks the 'Nailer's Quarter', with a wall of shelves holding the screws and nails.

Somers

A traditional miners' pub, the essence of country simplicity

When Richard Somers took on the pub in 1927, the Castlecomer coal mines were at their peak.

WHEN EDDIE SOMERS DIED IN December 2007, his family pub closed its doors after eighty years of distinguished service to the mining community who lived along 'the Ridge' between Castlecomer and the Carlow–Kilkenny border. The pub stands at the top of the hill in Clogh, close to a thatched cottage and a stone trough from which mules drank water a hundred years ago. Above the door is one word: 'SOMERS'. The plum-hued letters have been hanging there since Eddie's father, Richard, purchased the pub from the Walsh family in 1927, two years after the mighty Castlecomer coal seam was discovered. Richard had served as an apprentice barman in Roscrea and Portlaoise after the First World War and reckoned he was well suited to running a pub of his own.

The third of six children, Eddie was born above the pub shortly before Christmas 1931. He learned to read and write at the local school but, at the age of twelve, a bone infection caused his kidneys to fail. 'I was handicapped all my life but I always worked', insisted Eddie. 'I was never idle.' His first job was alongside his mother and father, cleaning taps, bottling the stout, keeping 'contrary' customers in order. When Richard died in 1954, Eddie's mother took over. The daughter of a Guinness cooper, she ran a tight ship until her own death in 1988, when Eddie stepped up to the mark.

Whether Somers pub will ever open again is not known. This is how it was in Eddie's day. A buzzy alarm rang when you entered. The main bar was a purely functional space, albeit decorated with pretty wallpaper. The floor was tiled simply to make it easy to mop. Customers either pulled up a stool or a bench or sat up at the bar itself. Nothing had changed in forty years. It was spotless. A stuffed fox beheld all, in Eddie's words 'nearly as old as myself, snared the year my father was married'. On the main wall was a poster of the Kilkenny Cats, Ireland's foremost hurling team, and a dartboard. 'We would have twelve or fourteen playing darts in a big way until maybe twenty years ago', said Eddie. A Tap Room to the right featured a piano, upon which Eddie's mother would play, and a fireplace. It was designed for dances and for women who 'wouldn't want to be seen'.

When Eddie first started at the pub, 'there was nothing, only coal characters here, horses and carts, and all miners'. Most of them were from mining stock for as far back

The late Eddie Somers doubled the family bar up as the central office for his thriving insurance business. His customers came from the mining families working the nearby Castlecomer coal mines.

Eddie's mother, Mary Somers, prided herself on the Guinness Extra Stout which she single-handedly bottled during the Guinness bicentenary of 1959.

as they knew. They were hard men who worked forty-five hours a week deep down in the dark, wet tunnels, hacking at the seams. In the winters they saw no daylight until Sunday. All they drank was bottled Guinness. 'They'd come here every Thursday, drink three small [bottles] and take six large ones home to have, one a day, with the dinner. I've lost twenty men like that in the last twenty years. They've all died now.'

Eddie Somers was a classic example of the 20th-century Irishman. Strong on tradition, dismissive of spongers, loyal to the Fianna Fáil party. He never found time for a wife or children. He was a regular Mass-goer. 'Faith is all I have. I don't see any better option and it never done me no harm. You won't get a smooth run in life.' He was also a passionate supporter of Kilkenny hurling. 'All my life, GAA got me out of all trouble. It kept me talking sport instead of more local things.'

Eddie became intimately acquainted with the local community through working in insurance, first alongside his father and subsequently on his own. Health insurance was a high priority with heart failure and emphysema common among the miners. Later they acted as money-lenders, enabling families to cover expenses of funerals and First Communions, or to purchase a Stanley cooker and tiles for the kitchen floor or outside toilets 'when the water came'. He learnt to be accurate early on. 'Father would always be a little careless. Maybe without his glasses, a few pence would be missing here and there.' Eddie, blessed with an in-built abacus, was always double-checking the sums in case they were asked to explain to 'the city lads' who were waiting for an excuse to 'make a show of you'. 'I made a resolution: they'll never make a show of me. If I made a mistake, I'd tear it up and start again.' His eyes shone when he talked figures, shillings and sixpences, percentages and additions and, above all, ways to increase one's money. 'It's all about management', he counselled.

The main bar consists of a tiled floor, a long radiator and pretty wallpaper. The only decoration is provided by posters of the Kilkenny Cats, generally considered Ireland's foremost hurling team.

When Eddie retired from the insurance business in 1988, he had nearly four hundred customers. He sold the business on and then, with tremendous sadness in his heart, emptied the press where he kept all his handwritten records and 'destroyed' them all. 'It was the only way. Once they were gone from me, they were out of mind.' The mines might have closed but Eddie could still draw a crowd until the end. 'The priest comes in of a Saturday night. We'd have no bad language here. An odd "feck" but you wouldn't mind that.' The customers converged at the bar to talk about matches past and coming soon. They were an honest crew. 'No credit. No boldness. No nothing at all.'

During the 1960s Eddie and his father also ran a hackney service, escorting past emigrants of Clogh to and from the ferry in Dublin. 'You'd be in the North Wall at seven o'clock when the boat come in. It was interesting work. It kept you in contact with people.' The same reasoning was behind his daily opening of Somers. 'For the first time in fifty-two years, I haven't any paperwork', he explained, a few months before his death. 'This is only a small pub. I keep it going just for the company now. But who knows, maybe they'll find another seam a hundred years from now and it'll all start over again.'

Eddie's orderly mind was exemplified by the deft manner in which he compartmentalized his till.

Mary Kennedy's

CALLAGHANE BRIDGE – CO. WATERFORD

The Kennedy family first opened a shebeen in their house in the 19th century

What shall we do with a drunken sailor, earl-eye in the morning?

The answer to certain regulars in Mary Kennedy's pub is obvious.

Heave him by the leg in a running bowline, earl-eye in the morning.

'Drunken Sailor' is probably the most famous of the traditional sea shanties to survive from the 19th century. Such songs were devised to help sailors achieve strenuous tasks like hoisting a sail or hauling in an anchor. The rhythm of the shanty songs enabled the crew to synchronize their movements, while simultanously imbuing them with a useful sense of good cheer and rum-fuelled optimism. The shantyman opened each verse; everyone else bellowed back the response.

In 2004, Mary Kennedy was asked whether she might open the back room of her small country pub as a practice venue for the nine-member Hooks and Crookes. The shanty group was formed in 2005 to entertain those gathering in Waterford to witness that summer's Tall Ships Race. Before long, they were performing at similar

Set in an Irish cottage, the pub features a pitched roof with reed thatch in the English style.

events from Newfoundland to Brittany. Every Monday night, the Hooks and Crookes meet at Kennedy's for unaccompanied practice, acapella renditions of 'Sailing in the Lowlands Low', 'Blood Red Roses' and such like.

Mary Kennedy's pub is to be found in a long, single-storey farm cottage some five miles south of Waterford City. Five elegantly shuttered windows and a series of pretty flower baskets break the monotony of the cottage's sallow, rendered walls. The roof is handsomely thatched. Flanking the cottage at either end stand the rubble-stone outbuildings and hay sheds which Mary's brother still uses for the family farm. Although a 'house and gardens' can be seen on this site on a mid-18th-century map, these buildings appear to date to the 1840s. Mary and her bricklayer husband, Ambrose 'Amby' Daniels, live in a new house to the rear.

The Kennedys were farmers from the Straits of Clashmore on the south coast of Waterford who settled by Callaghane Bridge in about 1855. The family lived in rooms at either end of the cottage but by the 1880s they were using a large room at the centre of the building as a shebeen. It would seem the lady of the house generally looked after this establishment. Mary's grandmother, Mary Jo Kennedy, certainly ran the show while her husband, Nicholas, kept his mind on the farm. Nicholas and Mary Jo had a large family but many died young. Of the survivors, Peg succeeded to the pub while Nicholas and Robbie, her brothers, took on the farm.

Mary Kennedy, the daughter of Nicholas, lost her mother when she was a child. As the eldest of five, she swiftly took on the mantle of responsibility, helping her father to cook and to clean their farm cottage. In time, Nicholas sent Mary to help out in the family pub. Peg had since passed away and Robbie, a bachelor, was in need of assistance serving drinks to the ever-increasing numbers coming to the pub. When Robbie died in 1979, Mary inevitably inherited the pub.

Customers sit upon old school benches set against wood-panelled walls.

The bar has occupied the very heart of the cottage since the 1880s.

FACING PAGE: A lampshade recalls the brilliance of local equine hero Dawn Run.

The pub currently consists of two rooms – a main bar, with red tile floors and pitch pine ceiling, and a back room where people play poker and the shanty singers practice. Seating options consist of five rattan stools, a handful of bentwood chairs and two school benches running along the walls. Radiators concealed beneath the benches add to the heat emanating from a pebbledash fireplace. Light from a converted cartwheel overhead and a pair of shell lamps bounces off copper coalscuttles and brass kettles. The walls are clad in tongue-and-groove to shoulder height, and are hung with paintings such as a copy of Vermeer's *The Letter* and a series by Peter Reddin. By the entrance hang photographs of race horses from the locality such as Limber Hill (Cheltenham Gold Cup, 1956), Freebooter (Aintree Grand National, 1950) and, above all, Dawn Run, the most successful race-mare in the history of National Hunt racing. Charmian Hill, the mare's owner, and her sons, Jeremy, Oliver and Barton, frequented Kennedy's in the glory days. Kennedy's thatch roof nearly blew clean off when Dawn Run completed the Cheltenham Gold Cup–Champion Hurdle double in 1986.

Traditionally, Kennedy's was a community pub where farmers and labourers from the parish came to drink, play poker and music and catch up on the gossip. Sometimes they came to fight. Fighting has, of course, been a phenomenon of the Irish countryside since earliest times. However, as Mary says, in those days people fought with bare fists rather than knives and guns. She recalls many a brawl breaking out in the family pub: 'Fellows were always turning the tables over.' Her crafty solution was to commission a local joiner to make three new tables with iron bases so weighty that you would need to sing a particularly vigorous shanty in order to tip them up.

Many country pubs in Ireland do not open because the families who own them no longer live there. The Kennedys still live next to their pub but do not open until the late afternoon because daytime business is too sporadic these days. Nonetheless, Mary does her bit to promote trade, hosting the shanty sessions and the occasional pub quiz. She understands that for the pub to survive, she will probably have to make some far-reaching changes to the essence of the establishment. She does not expect any of her own children to take on the pub, encouraging them instead to make their mark in their own respective professions.

RIGHT: A gnarly fox is set to leap into a picnic hamper above the bar in the Butterfly Room. Installed in the early 1980s, the bar already looks a century older. Fishing rods sprawl across the ceiling.

ABOVE: The fireplace was made of bricks salvaged from Peacock's General Store in Limerick. Along the overmantel are metal pressed nameplates of local residents of a bygone age – the landlord, Captain Vansittart of Coolbawn, and tradesmen J. Duffy and T. Stoney. Sandwiched between whiskey urns above the fireplace is a glass box, by Bobby Duick, containing figurines of four traditional musicians who play here on Wednesday nights.

P. J. Guerin
(The Kingfisher)

CASTLECONNELL – CO. LIMERICK

A woman once came in to ask for directions and ended up staying four years

FOR PADDY GUERIN, COACHES HAVE NEVER been far from his mind. His father and grandfather were coachbuilders from Limerick City. With a few essential tools and their own bare hands, they could make 'anything on wheels – tub traps, hearses, floats, carts, carriages, you name it'. As a young man, Paddy himself collaborated on the making of the last stagecoach for the President of Ireland. His entire bespectacled frame shifts excitedly as he explains the intricacies of the job. However, as cars became more commonplace, Paddy tired of the sport, closed down the business and bought himself a pub.

In 1815, Carlo Bianconi, a young Italian print-seller living in Ireland, single-handedly revolutionized the island's transport system when he established the first regular horse-drawn carriage service. Within a few years, Bianconi inns and coach houses were to be found along virtually every main road in the land. In 1978, Paddy and his new wife, Mary Beacom, purchased one of these former coach houses. It stood in Castleconnell, a pretty fishing resort near Limerick City, on the banks of the river Shannon. At its peak, the village had eight hotels offering cool linen sheets and weighty woollen blankets to the well-to-do who came here with tackle and rod. The local economy boomed until the 1930s when a new dam dramatically reduced both the levels and the flow of the river. Fishing went into decline and today there is just one hotel, a former convent, now principally used for wedding receptions.

Paddy was not the first publican in the family. 'Edward Lane', the name of his mother's father, was emblazoned in marble letters over a large premises in Limerick City's milk market. Edward was 'the last of the big league tailors in Limerick', says Paddy. His premises also contained 'a pub with big high windows' and a fishing shop. It was fishing that brought Paddy to Castleconnell. When he was 'only a small lad', a family friend by the name of Peter O'Callaghan took him on the first of many adventures up the Shannon, pointing out the wildlife as they passed – a Whooper swan here, a kingfisher there. Paddy's fascination with nature extends into his pub, home to a fine collection of stoats, squirrels, mallards, pheasants, sparrowhawks, kestrels and foxes, stuffed by local taxidermists P. J. Kenny and Tony Griffin. Fortunately, despite the taming of the river, there remain a few explosions of rumbling rapids and leaping

Peculiar characters appear in every nook and cranny.

A dining table with its mismatched chairs stands ready for stout, whiskey and playing cards.

cataracts that appeal to salmon. On one wall hangs a remarkable salmon, 24 pounds (10.8 kg) in weight, caught on a home-made brass spoon lure in 1999.

In a glass box above the main fireplace, four traditional musicians are at play on red velvet seats with fiddles, whistles and bodhráns. The figurines were designed by a French woman who called into Paddy's pub one night looking for directions. She ended up staying four years. Each figurine represents one of the local musicians who gather at the Kingfisher on Wednesday evenings for a session.

You can still see the arches in the wall into which the Bianconi coaches reversed at night to unload bags and valuables. A trapdoor in the ceiling provided the only access to the drivers' bedrooms. The loops through which horses were tied up for the night are still on the backyard walls. In the 1930s, the pub passed from the Lee family to Paddy Scanlan, goalkeeper for the Limerick team that won the All-Ireland Senior Hurling Championships in 1934, 1936 and 1940. The hurling legends Mick and John Mackey lived next door.

Paddy's pub offers perhaps a dozen different seating arrangements: flowery sofas, quirky bar stools, upturned half-casks, railway benches, church pews and rough wooden tables, everything is different. Paddy also converted the property into

a place to store the things that he had collected. 'I'm like a crow. I pick up things. Everything is borrowed, never given back or stolen.' He is particularly proud of a three-tiered glass box full of peculiar objects – a drawknife for shaving timber, a tea-strainer, a nutcracker, a tie-press, a rifle cleaner and scales for weighing gold – and is fond of getting people to try and guess what the objects are. Fishing rods sprawl across the roof. In the back room, a massive butterfly cabinet takes centre stage while the shelves around are laden with old cash tills, donkey collars, bog oak carvings, fishing nets, photos of beloved drinkers and great catches past. Every light bulb is daubed with paint to keep the ambience calm – 'you don't want to dazzle people but I tell them it's to save electricity!'

In a small room at the back, Paddy has a tackle shop selling rods, flies and spinners, and arranges outings with resident ghillie Mick O'Doherty. When not selling rods or pulling pints, Paddy is actively involved in trying to get the surrounding area classified as a nature reserve. It is a race against time; Castleconnell's core is changing rapidly. 'The village will double in size over the next five years', he says. 'There's 1,400 new houses under construction at the now. I have no problem with progress so long as it's in the character of the village.'

Wall features include two of the cartridges fired as part of the gun salute when John F. Kennedy arrived in Ireland in 1963.

129

O'Shaughnessy's (The Ivy House)

GLIN – CO. LIMERICK

Choose your chair in this blend of Irish tradition and Hungarian aesthetics

THERE IS A STORY ABOUT A KNIGHT OF Glin who, during an assault on his castle by an English fleet, had one of his sons captured. A message was sent to the Knight stating that if he did not surrender, his son would be blasted from the ship's cannon against the castle walls. The Knight is said to have replied: 'Fire away, there's plenty more where he came from!'

What became of the unfortunate son is not recorded but it's the sort of legend that must have appealed to Dody Meer when she came to roost in a pub by the walls of Glin Castle in 1952. Dody's Hungarian homeland had been devastated by the loss of seventy-one per cent of its territory in the wake of the First World War. For Dody's father, Leo, a banker and stockbroker in Budapest, the situation became intolerable. In May 1939, he sent his daughter to holiday with friends in Essex, where she stayed until the Second World War was over. In due course, she was joined by Leo who, as well as being a banker, was a brilliant musician, playing viola with the London Philharmonic Orchestra. In later life, he would sit in the blue sitting room above O'Shaughnessy's bar and practice for six hours straight.

In 1946, Dody visited her cousin and his wife, Pixie, in Surrey, England. Pixie was an O'Shaughnessy from a mysterious land called Limerick in the farthest reaches of Ireland. Her brother John was also present, a tall man and a Captain in the Irish army.

Both the back bar and counter were salvaged in the 1960s from Liston's chemists in Limerick.

Dody and the Captain exchanged words and smiles and fell in love. They were married in London in 1948.

A squash racquet and a carpet beater frame a travelling priest's altar from penal times, found in New York.

The O'Shaughnessys descend from Sir Dermot O'Shaughnessy, a warrior from Gort in Co. Galway knighted during the reign of Henry VIII. A branch has been in Glin since 1692. In the late 19th century, 'Old Pat' O'Shaughnessy, second cousin of the aforementioned Captain, acquired a single-storey building on the village's Market Square. As was customary at the time, he ran the business as a grocer, hardware store, building supplier and public house. Pat ran the business with his only son, Maurice, a haemophiliac. After the latter's premature death, Pat engaged his cousin Mossy to help out. In his will, Old Pat left young Mossy both his pub and some considerable debts. Mossy was also a cousin of Captain Con Colbert who commanded the rebels at the Jameson Distillery during the Easter Rising. Colbert was subsequently court-martialled and shot, declaring, 'Better a dead man, than a live coward!' shortly before the fatal guns fired. His death inevitably caused unrest in Glin and the town experienced its share of trouble in the ensuing War of Independence.

FACING PAGE: *Old whiskey jars and photographs from the Lawrence Collection adorn the upper shelves of the main bar.*

Colourful rugs and tablecloths give the former kitchen a cheerful lilt.

In Mossy's time, the pub was known as The Ivy House due to the green leaves creeping up its walls. A room to one side of the pub was sublet as an office to a travelling solicitor who came to Glin once a week to resolve local disputes. Mossy ran the pub until his premature demise during a botched hospital operation in 1952. As he left no will, all his siblings had an equal claim. Ultimately they all signed their claim over to the youngest sibling, Captain John O'Shaughnessy, of the Irish Army.

John returned from London in 1952, his wife and sons following later. It must have been an astonishing time for Dody to move from London to an isolated community in rural Ireland where transport was scarce and foreigners somewhat marvelled at for their fancy notions of indoor loos and the like.

Assisted by a German friend, she set up one of the first cottage industries in Ireland, teaching villagers the intricacies of basket-making and rush-ware. A tremendous comfort was a telephone in the house. Dody's son Thomas O'Shaughnessy recalls an endless stream of farmers subsequently calling by on the way to the creamery, asking him to dial '11' to get the vet out for their sick animals.

By 1960, Dody's keen Magyar tastes had deduced that the only hope for the somewhat drab interior of her husband's pub lay in a complete revamp. The Captain was all in favour although, as Thomas points out, Dody was always close at hand 'to keep him on the straight and narrow'. The Captain, though universally loved as a fine gentleman and a marvellous storyteller, clearly had questionable aesthetic sensibilities.

Both the Captain and his father, Maurice, were Secretary and Chairman of the Glin Coursing Club. Coursing took place out 'over the far-famed Glin demesne' with substantial stake money to be won. The pub's close affiliation with coursing is attested to by the greyhound resting above its entrance. The Captain's cousin Pat was one of the pub's great characters. He tended to live in the kitchen and liked to put cubes of butter into his tea instead of milk. Indeed, he held court from an armchair carefully placed within a vast timber box formerly used for holding parts for Ford motorcars. He also frequently slept there.

After Pat's death, Dody converted the kitchen into a delightful room where musical sessions now take place around the nimble Monington & Weston piano. The mighty Liscannor flagstone floors, salvaged from a Catholic church in Old Pat's time, were given a lift when the surrounding walls were painted in bright and cheerful colours. A traditional clevvy (a type of kitchen cabinet or dresser) is now laden with cups and pretty vases of wild flowers and miscellaneous oddities. Drinkers recline in a variety of country chairs, from armchairs to

sticklebacks, resting their drinks on simple kitchen tables. Beautifully produced greyhound posters unfurl alongside shelves stacked with ledger books and fifteen volumes of Greyhound Stud Books. A ceiling beam is festooned with a bee helmet, a scythe, a gas lamp, a garland of party balloons, and a stray boot made at the old Christian Brothers industrial school in Glin. Alongside a butter churn and a stuffed otter are framed photographs of Con Colbert and pictures of fellow Irish patriots Robert Emmet and Daniel O'Connell. A poster relates the tolls and charges for bringing goods to market in Glin during Old Pat's day.

Above the hearth is a travelling priest's altar from penal times, complete with anointment water, crucifix, holy water spoon and embroidered cloth. Somehow this remarkable piece had made it to New York where it was discovered by Thomas's brother Jancsi and brought home again. 'I used to work in a museum in London', laughs Thomas's wife, Val. 'And now I'm living in one.'

Thomas and Val took on the family pub in 2002. They live in a nearby house with two teenage sons. Thomas, half-Magyar, half-Limerick, has a full-time job with an independent oil and chemical storage company in Foynes. He opens the pub only on Friday evenings, at weekends and on certain mornings. He has no intention of selling. 'O'Shaughnessy was the name above the bar when I got it. And it'll be the name above it when I go', he says. 'That's all I can do.'

A chart reveals the escalating cost of a pint of stout from 1900 to the present day.

FACING PAGE: *Liscannor flagstones lead past old bridles and kegs to the gentlemen's toilets.*

M. Finucane

In the past, customers would come in for a drink and a new suit

The ceiling above the Columbian pine bar is festooned with dressage collars, bicycle pedals, army garters and a carbide carriage lamp.

LATE IN THE EVENING OF FRIDAY, 28 April 1916, Michael Joseph O'Rahilly dragged his bullet-riddled body into a doorway off Dublin's Moore Street and lay down. Before he died, the Kerryman managed a short letter 'written after I was shot' to his 'darling Nancy'. He explained his predicament to her, sent 'tons & tons of love dearie to you & the boys & to Nell & Anna'. 'It was a good fight anyhow', he concluded. 'Goodbye Darling.' 'The O'Rahilly' (as he styled himself) was the only leader of the Easter Rising to die in action. As he prepared to meet his executioners the following week, Padraig Pearse said, 'I envy O'Rahilly – that is the way I wanted to die'. If they make a movie of the rising of 1916, the actor who gets The O'Rahilly's part can be sure of a dramatic finale.

The O'Rahilly was born in 1875 at his father's pub in Ballylongford. The small north Kerry town lies along the most westerly banks of the river Shannon. Michael O'Rahilly built the two-storey pub in 1809; its Columbian pine floor dates to this period. By 1861, his entrepreneurial grandson, Richard O'Rahilly, had expanded the business to such an extent that he was variously described as baker, draper, grocer, fish curer, miller, farmer, landowner, importer, inventor, post office manager, shipping agent, general merchant and, perhaps most importantly, publican. Richard is even said to have had the first refrigerator in Ireland. He was undoubtedly the wealthiest man in the area. When he died in 1896 he left his estate to his wife, Ellen, and his business to his son Michael.

Where Richard was a prudent investor, loyal to the Crown, his son and heir was a deeply compulsive man whose opinions were increasingly at odds with the British forces in Ireland. In 1898, Michael sold his father's businesses in Ballylongford and sailed for New York with an engagement ring in his pocket. In April the following year, he married his 'darling Nancy'.

A life-size portrait of The O'Rahilly hangs today on the wall of the public house which he briefly owned, surrounded by photographs of his De Dion-Bouton car, a copy of the letter he wrote to Nancy, the Proclamation of 1916 and images of other rebel leaders. The association with O'Rahilly inevitably meant the pub became something of a stronghold for Republican get-togethers during the formative years of the new state. Indeed, one man well known in Finucane's was Dan Keating who, at the time of his death in 2007, was the oldest man in Ireland. Keating, a veteran of the War of Independence, liked to address the pub's owner, Michael Finucane, as 'The Young O'Rahilly'.

Michael Finucane is a large man with an easy smile and warm handshake. Before he took on the pub, he worked as a builder on the mighty factories and power stations that dominate the skyline along this part of the Shannon. He is not, as it happens, any relation of The O'Rahilly. His great-uncle Mike Finucane, purchased the pub from the rebel leader in 1898 with money made working on the American

A full-length photograph of 'The O'Rahilly', the 1916 rebel leader, hangs behind an old National cash register.

The walls of the piano room host a collection of old-fashioned advertisements and signposts.

railroads during his youth. Mike ran the pub as a drapery and grocery-bar until his death in 1942. As he had no children, he left the pub to his nephew, also called Michael Finucane, who ran it with his wife, Ellen, a schoolteacher, for the next forty years. When Michael Finucane II died in 1982, the pub passed to the present owner, Michael Finucane III. 'We've not had to change the name over the door in a long time', says Michael.

Michael has done much to ensure his pub remains an aesthetic delight. An overhead shelf runs around the room, groaning under the weight of tobacco-stained footballs, whiskey jars, tumblers, brass lamps, ash plant canes and fishing nets. Cheerful green leather stools assemble along the Columbian pine bar and miscellaneous oddities hang from the ceiling above. A pair of forty-gallon hogsheads behind the bar recall a time when publicans watered down whiskey to suit the tastes of their customers. Among the photographs on the walls, pride of place is given to Michael's late uncle, Father Donal Bambury, bestowing his blessing on the first Sunday race meeting in England at Doncaster. In a snug to the rear, shelves cascade with further peculiarities – a 1930s builder's helmet, a Bush radio, a banker's coin-checker, an album by The Pecker Dunne and a coathanger 'stolen from the House of Lords'.

'Bally' was once a thriving town with two creameries and a massive corn mill. At the back of the pub stands a series of whitewashed buildings and a storehouse with a hatch that leads directly onto a small riverside pier. In The O'Rahilly's day, barges pulled in at this pier, laden with twenty-stone sacks of flour, drapery cloth and general cargo from Limerick. Horses and carts were also at the ready to transport large quantities of salted herring, mackerel and salmon, stored in barrels of salt, to the railway station at Listowel and from there to Dublin.

During the 1980s, both creameries closed and the corn mill followed suit. The north Kerry farmers found themselves increasingly short of excuses to journey in to 'Bally'. Only during the week of the Listowel Races would the seaside town become busy. The younger generations began to emigrate in droves to New York, beckoned by useful connections with a former Ballylongford man who had already risen to the upper echelons of the New York trade unions.

Finucane's pub still had a grocery and drapery attached when Michael was a youngster. At one end of the bar counter is the yardstick used by the in-house tailors to measure arm lengths. Customers would sit at the bar and drink a pint or two, while their tailor proposed different colours and cloths. 'People had more time then', explains Michael. 'It was very civilized.' The rise of superstores in the 1960s brought an end to the drapery and the grocery section met a similar fate a decade later.

Michael is not one to sit about waiting for customers. Aided by his wife, Deirdre, and several stalwart friends, they have ensured the pub remains the epicentre of life for the surrounding community. Michael claims he would know 'every seed, breed and generation of them'. His 26-year-old son, Micheál IV, concurs. 'The customers are like your family. I could name the time they'd come in, where they'd sit and what they'd order.' The pub opens only in the evening but is frequently packed. Michael is settling into a lifestyle of fishing, shooting and the occasional boating jaunt around the estuary to Ballybunion. 'I've a bit of land out the way and I do a bit of gardening.' He cultivates oysters out in the harbour and is one of the co-organizers of the annual Ballylongford Oyster Festival. The town hosts a Summer Festival in honour of the poet Brendan Kennelly. A touching poem Kennelly wrote on the death of Michael's mother, Ellen, is framed on the pub wall.

Micheál IV currently works in financial services and is debating whether to take on the family business. Having grown up in a pub, he understands what that might entail. His father believes he might be better off sticking to stocks and bonds. 'I wouldn't blame him – it's a tough life.'

BELOW, LEFT: *The week of the Listowel Races encourages a considerable rise in trade for the pubs of north Kerry.*

BELOW: *Old advertisements and hobnail boots hang above the bar.*

O'Loclainn's

This hotel first became popular with motorists in the Edwardian Age

FACING PAGE: *Formerly owned by Dylan Thomas's father-in-law, O'Loclainn's is a welcome pit-stop for anyone passing through the glorious Burren landscape.*

IN 1022, EIGHT YEARS AFTER BRIAN BORU defeated the Vikings at Clontarf, Ireland experienced a brief interregnum during which the two 'regents', Cuán O'Loclainn, the chief poet, and Corcoran, a cleric, ran the country. Little is known of either man save that Cuán, a distinguished scholar who wrote a poem about the palace at Tara, was assassinated just two years later. According to the *Annals of Tighernach*, 'the party that killed him became putrid within the hour', a vengeance known as 'a poet's miracle'. Nonetheless, Cuán's descendants flourished and, by the 15th century, the O'Loughlins (O'Loclainn) had established themselves as the most powerful family in north-west Clare. They bore the title 'Kings of Burren', presiding over that mystical, magical Burren limestone landscape, with castles all along the shore of the Atlantic and Galway Bay.

In 1653, Cromwell's New Model Army finally achieved victory in a long and gruelling campaign against the Irish Confederacy. Some 12,000 Cromwellian veterans were awarded land confiscated from the Irish in lieu of pay. The O'Loclainns' territory was seized and granted to the Duke of Buckingham. He allowed the O'Loclainns to retain full use of the land in return for a nominal rent. In the late 19th century, these same lands passed to Colonel Henry White,

later Baron Annaly, son of a Dublin bookseller who secured a vast personal fortune operating the state lottery. Annaly seems to have quadrupled the rent on his lands and subsequently evicted the O'Loclainns of Newtown Cashel for non-payment.

Small wonder, then, that Peter J. O'Loclainn should ally himself with the causes of nationalism and republicanism in the early years of the 20th century. In the summer of 1918, he was elected first Sinn Féin chairman of Co. Clare. Inevitably, Peter became a target during the War of Independence. In 1920, the Black and Tans, a

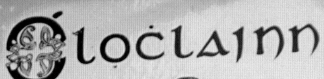

IRISH
WHISKEYS

notoriously ill-disciplined reserve police force, threatened to burn his house unless he carried out certain orders. 'I do not believe I can have your order complied with', replied Peter. 'In any event I'm not going to try. So don't wait twenty-four hours: start burning now.' The soldiers carved 'God Save the King' in his hallway and marched away for a rethink.

During the 1920s, Peter became an intimate colleague of Eamon de Valera,

Glass cabinets, laughing cavaliers and welcome radiators rise up the dark wood-panelled walls.

Ireland's first Taoiseach (prime minister), holding an important position on Ireland's first banking commission. From 1938 to 1944, he held a seat in the Dáil, the Irish Parliament, and he was later elected to the Irish Senate. Away from politics, Peter ran a large shop at Monks in Ballyvaughan where he operated as a tea, wine and bacon merchant, selling basic grocery goods, hardware, animal feed and fertilizer. One of his core businesses was the supply of coal to lighthouses along the surrounding coastline. He also purchased pigs from a large factory in Limerick and, as agent for Guinness, supplied all the local pubs with stout.

In 1935, Peter's sons, MacNeill and Eamon, purchased MacNamara's Hotel in Ballyvaughan. The hotel, formerly owned by Dylan Thomas's father-in-law, dated to the 1840s and featured in many 19th-century guidebooks. The thirteen-bedroom hotel, known today as O'Loclainn's, was originally a stop off for horse coaches but, with the advent of automobiles, became popular with motorists. An enamel endorsement by the AA's forerunner, the Motoring Union of Britain & Ireland, hangs outside the pub door today.

MacNeill O'Loclainn and his wife, May, lived in the old hotel with their five children. They ran the business as a bar and grocery, supplying newspapers to the parish. 'Mac' also concentrated on running the family's dairy farm, which they had regained since Irish independence. From 1995, his eldest son, Peter, took an increasingly active role in the business and, upon Mac's death in 2000, Peter succeeded to O'Loclainn's.

Today, this intimate traditional bar in the tiny Burren village represents one of the finest establishments on the west coast. It also boasts a connoisseur's selection of whiskeys. Peter's father is credited with the hypnotic range on display, now numbering over three hundred golden bottles, including rare breeds from several distillers that have long ceased to exist. Peter confesses that he prefers stout to whiskey but his counsel on the subject is constantly sought and the man certainly knows his subject exceedingly well.

Peter was born above the bar and now lives in the old hotel bedrooms with his wife, Margaret, and two children. He remembers life here as 'a young lad'. 'There would be seven or eight people drinking here all day, every day. Where they got the money from, I don't know. Some did have money, more didn't. But they'd sell their potatoes or their cattle and they'd come in and pay it all off.'

In 1996, Peter recruited designer Angela Murphy to incorporate a new fireproof ceiling and to rearrange the interior. The bar counter was shifted one way and the rusty greengrocer drawers, redundant since the advent of supermarkets, were placed to the back. Scotch pine boards run up each wall, then yield to painted brick upon which hangs a series of ash-framed photographs of local characters by Veronica Nicholson. The view from the window beholds Galway Bay and a meadow of stumpy ash trees. The landscape to the south is an ancient, sometimes eerie plateau of unusual flora, limestone caves and burial tombs. The whole effect is dark, inspiring and immaculately clean. If Cuán O'Loclainn was to return to earth in pursuit of a place to write some further stanzas, he would be hard pushed to beat the pub now run by his lineal descendant.

The original bar was extended during the 1990s when the owner converted the grocery section to house one of the finest whiskey collections west of the Shannon.

Murray's

A quiet pub by day, it evolves a mischievous persona the instant darkness falls

'LET SCHOOLMASTERS PUZZLE THEIR BRAIN with grammar and nonsense and learning', scoffed Oliver Goldsmith. 'Good liquor, I stoutly maintain, gives genius a better discerning.' The son of a clergyman, Goldsmith spent an idyllic childhood in a parsonage near the 'deserted village' of 'sweet Auburn' on the border between Counties Longford and Westmeath. Described as 'impenetrably stupid' by his first teacher, this 'small, lumpish' man with a 'lively, sad, ugly face' is today hailed as one of the most remarkable literary figures of the 18th century. His monument, sculpted by John Henry Foley, stands outside Trinity College Dublin.

The landscape that inspired Goldsmith to write his classic poems ('The Deserted Village'), stirring novels (*The Vicar of Wakefied*) and graceful plays (*She Stoops to Conquer*) was the countryside he knew as a child. It extended westwards over bumpy bog roads, rich pastures and diminutive streams to the sloping shores of Lough Ree, the second largest lake in the Irish midlands. One of the small hamlets lying along the lake is Maghera, whose name is derived from the Irish Machaire Rátha, meaning 'plain of the ring-fort'.

At the heart of this remote community stands Murray's old-style bar, a whitewashed 18th-century cottage with an asbestos roof, boasting one the smallest bars in the land. Behind the counter stands Lizzie, the fourth generation of the Murray women to run the bar. Lizzie, who was born here, inherited the pub upon the death of her mother in 2002. Her husband, a farmer, keeps cattle and sheep in fields to the back of the pub.

Lizzie believes the pub started as a shebeen some three hundred years ago. The Murrays have been there since at least 1823 when a forefather was laid to rest in the local graveyard. The pub was as simple then as it is now, a straightforward drinking den. In the days of her grandmother, there was a small grocery attached, 'for tea, sugar, maybe a loaf of bread', but today it is straight-up drink.

Above the bar counter hangs an anonymous quotation with considerable appeal to the bachelors who drink at Murray's: 'When a man is single, he lives at his ease. He don't give a damn and does as he please.' To breathe, a pub should swell with its own personality, even when everyone's gone home. Murray's has that look about it.

An ostensibly quiet pub by day, it evolves a mischievous persona the instant darkness falls. Everything that seemed stationary bristles with life. Chairs, stools and chequered tables start shuddering with anticipation.

As Lizzie says, you really do need to be here at night to get 'the real tone of it'. On Thursdays and Sundays, musicians take a pew beside the old turf-burning stove and set up a jig that soon has 'the auld lads and auld lasses out there dancing'. Her father was a keen singer in the generation past. Of course, business has quietened somewhat since the drink-driving laws came in but, as a man at the bar says, there is nothing to stop you getting close by boat.

'An old house likes old colours', says Lizzie, who chose the khaki greens and russet earthy colours because she felt they would absorb the hue of her customers' tobacco. An overhead strip light radiates off the pitch pine floor and ceiling, rippling along the brown bottles of cider, larger and ale stocked behind the bar. On a shelf above, three Kilbeggan whiskey jars are in deep conversation with a rare bottle of the ill-fated Guinness Bitter. A poster for 'Lizzie's Lotto' promises a small fortune but everyone knows that the winner will most likely be obliged to buy them all a drink. A barometer symbolically indicates that there is no pressure at all. Photographs of smartly dressed characters who drank here half a century ago are juxtaposed between

a song sheet for 'Danny Boy', a Bridget's cross and the Sacred Heart of Jesus. On another wall hang various prints collected down the years – a J. W. Gozzard landscape, a wren by F. Toole, set-dancing by A. C. Pape, John Everett Millais's portrait of pretty Eveline Lees.

'I have my own trade from round about. Every evening we have a certain amount but a good few come in on a Friday night.' In the wintertime, local farmers and fishermen gather around the stove, frequently clasping playing cards in their paws. The subject of conversation often concerns the number of eels dwelling in the shallow freshwaters of Lough Ree. Traditionally many of these families depended on eel fishing for their livelihood, particularly for those who once lived upon the lake's islands. In 1960, three clergymen espied an immense eel that fitted the description of 'a great conger eel, seven yards long, and as thick as a bull in the body with a mane on its back like a horse' recorded by 19th-century folklorist Thomas Croker. Inevitably, the sighting has inspired comparisons with Loch Ness although this particular monster has not been seen again for nearly half a century.

'Some days I open at eleven o'clock', says Lizzie. 'On others, I'll wait until twelve. There's always work to do and when we have one bit done, then we have another bit to do. But I'll always open because there's always someone popping around.'

Floral stools run the length of the narrow green bar room, encouraging intimate banter between customer and landlady.

Coyle & Sons

FOUR ROADS – CO. ROSCOMMON

This converted grainstore has been serving drinks since the 19th century

LIAM OG COYLE TAKES UP HIS HURLING stick, faces the bar and, with tremendous concentration furrowing his brow, roars: 'Goo-woo'. At the age of two, Liam is not really in a position to delve any further into the subject. His younger brother charges past in a baby-walker and slams straight into a wrought-iron radiator. Simon Coyle cups his chin and nose in both hands in an effort to regain some sort of fatherly command over it all.

'I am the fourth generation', he says. 'And these two are the fifth.' The two-storey limestone building that is Coyle's pub has been in the family since 1840. At least, that was the year when Simon's great-grandfather, William Coyle, is said to have settled at Four Roads. It can't have been a thriving community at the time. A survey of 1837 says Four Roads consisted of a solitary chapel and 'a small thatched house in bad repair'. The 'four roads' in question may have ultimately led to Roscommon, Galway, Athlone and Ballinasloe, but this was nonetheless a secondary crossroads. A crossroads in the middle of nowhere. Initially, William may have simply used the building as a grainstore. However, he was soon struck by the notion that the farming families of the parish might like a place to purchase basic amenities and to meet for a drink. It apparently took seven years before he opened his grocery-bar and, by then, the Great Famine had begun. Nonetheless, he and his wife, Ellen, pressed on and, by the 1860s, Coyle's had become a landmark establishment for the Suck valley. Indeed, the crossroads was soon busy enough to warrant the opening of a second pub by a family called Kelly on one of the other corners.

It is in pubs such as Coyle's and Kelly's that plots are hatched and loyalties sworn. When two-year-old Liam Og wields his stick like that, it is because he is imbued with the spirit of a great and proud hurling tradition. The hurlers of Four Roads, also known as Tisrara, have won twenty-nine of Co. Roscommon's Senior Hurling Championship titles since the club's foundation in 1905. That achievement leaves them a long way ahead of their rivals and spurred them on to victory again in 2005. The team practise in the pump field behind Kelly's pub where Sunday games took

FACING PAGE AND ABOVE:
Constructed with limestone and brick, Coyle's has been in the same family since 1840.

The pitch pine counter in the main bar was salvaged from the staircase of an abandoned convent.

place right into the 1960s. Great crowds would gather to watch and a single match might last from two o'clock until well after six o'clock. One commentator suggests 'there may have been over twenty-a-side at times, with lads joining in and departing at different times'.

By the time William's son Simon took on the business in the late 19th century, the Coyles were supplying spirits, hardware, drapery, bootware, coffins, habits, groceries, seeds and manure. They also bottled their own porter and distributed it among the local farmers. When the bottles returned, they had to keep an eye on them to see what other purposes they'd been used for in the meantime. More often than not, they were tainted with oil. In 1964, Simon's son Liam Coyle began a courtship with Ellen Kelly, daughter of his neighbouring publican. The couple married soon after and Liam established a machinery yard to the back of Kelly's pub. When Ellen's mother became ill soon after, the young couple took over the running of the pub. Things became more complex when Liam's father died and he inherited Coyle's pub. Realistically, with Ireland enduring an economic downturn during the 1970s, there could be only one pub at the crossroads. Kelly's closed for business in 1980 and is today a derelict building, up for sale. Coyle's continued the grocery until the late 1980s but that too had fizzled out by the time Simon Coyle took on the pub in 1992.

Over the past few years, Simon and his wife, Breata, have brought the pub back to the way it was. A hundred years of paint and plaster have been chipped away from doors, windows and shelves to reveal the original timber fittings. The Liscannor slate floor has been cleaned and polished. The pitch pine ceiling was salvaged from Kelly's pub, as were two of the doors. The bar was crafted using timber that formerly held up the stairs of an old convent.

Simon has by no means finished his refurbishment yet but vows that he will 'never change the heart of it'. He has plans for a restaurant, a car park and a beer garden and hopes to place antiques throughout. 'Anything I put in will be old', he says. If the back bar is anything to go by, he is on the right track. Shelf upon shelf stacked with brass jugs, hurling trophies and an original ticket for the 1972 Croke Park showdown between Muhammad Ali and Al 'Blue' Lewis. Old ale advertisements and photographs of the Four Roads hurling champions are echoed in a heavily blotched mirror. The old lodge books are buttressed by dusty bottles of Pot Still Whiskey and gripe water. The old Tap Room next door also impresses with its collection of suitcases, clay pipes, gas lamps and an Edwardian clock from the International Time Recording Company. A Bakelite switch ignites the gentlemen's loo, a fine sanctuary of Belfast sink, stainless steel taps and exposed brickwork.

Shelves above the bar are stacked with cobwebby machinery, soda siphons and old gripe-water bottles.

'I started out filling boxes of grocery for my grandmother in Kelly's', says Simon. 'Filling bags of snuff and clove drops and tea.' He pulled his first pint when he was five years old. 'It cost 16 pence and I could tell you the time and nearly the day that I poured it.' The recipient was a particularly cantankerous off-duty Garda. 'He tasted it and didn't like it and reared on me.' Fortunately, Simon's father arrived on the scene and swiftly threw the Garda out. Simon chanced upon the same officer some twenty years later while working as a bartender in a Dublin pub. Simon poured him his pint and said: 'I hope that's better than the last one I gave you.' The Garda considered him for a while and then remembered. 'You're young Coyle from Four Roads.'

'I've had days when I'd like to have pulled out', concedes Simon. 'But this is what I've known all my life. For some reason, I get a great buzz behind the counter. I've never done anything else. And I wouldn't sell it for twenty million.'

Leonard's

The counter tops were salvaged from an abandoned ship in Belfast harbour

FACING PAGE: *The grocery shelves are stocked with breakfast cereals, biscuits and cleaning products.*

BELOW: *A box by the entrance advises passers-by of upcoming funerals.*

LEONARD'S PUB STANDS IN THE SMALL village of Lahardane, midway between the towns of Crossmolina and Pontoon. A patchwork of conifer plantations, brown-green bogs and sheep-speckled pastures runs eastwards towards the shores of Lough Conn. The soaring slopes of Nephin Mor ascend to the west.

The story begins in 1897 when it was built as a two-storey guesthouse by a gentleman called Cadden who sold it to the Durcan family during the 1920s. In 1943, Laurence Leonard gave up his career at McIntyre's wholesalers in Belmullet and bought the pub. His wife, Molly Kearns, worked in Joseph Murphy's hardware store in Ballina. The Leonards duly opened a grocery section, offering sheep-farming families from the community a useful array of tea, sweets, boots, shoes, hardware, seeds, wine, spirits and beer.

Twenty-three years after he took on the pub, Laurence passed away leaving Molly with seven children, 'two lads and five girls'. 'She was a busy woman', says J. P., her youngest child, who came home from Blackrock College, Dublin, to help his mother in 1976. When Molly passed away in 2006, J. P. and his wife, Helen, inherited the premises. The Leonards now live above the pub and have a son and three daughters.

Although Leonard's is one of the few 'originals' left in Mayo, the family-run pub has been almost entirely renovated over the past nine years. 'All that was left of the actual building were the four walls', says J. P., with considerable feeling. 'The whole place was banjaxed. So we started from the ceiling and worked our way down. We had to fit in new panelling, new stair-boards, a new ceiling, but everything was put back exactly as it was . . . well, nearly everything.' An impractically small snug with its own private fireplace was incorporated into the main bar. The 'beauty board' (a board punctured with rows of small holes) his father put behind the bar was too much of a dust magnet to remain. The cement floor was replaced with sturdy flagstones.

The principal room is a broad, mustard-hued enclave, with flagstone floor and a tongue-and-groove ceiling. The structure is just as it was in Larry Leonard's day – a long bar counter on the left, a shorter grocery counter and shelves on the right. Much of the 'new' woodwork is in fact reused from elsewhere. All three pitch pine counter tops were salvaged from an abandoned ship in Belfast harbour. The panelling around the fireplace came from an old school in Massbrook and the main doors from a derelict hotel in Swinford. The original sash windows were either renovated or reconstructed by Carrabine Joinery of Ballina. Local carpenter Jim Fahy was on hand to build the grocery shelves and sliding-door cabinets. Helen Leonard added the overhead lamps and came up with the idea of installing a wheel from an old hay-cart into a porthole, adding a contemporary twist.

Resting on one shelf are the carefully kept ledgers of Laurence Leonard from the time he purchased the pub in 1943 until his death in 1966. 'I'm afraid his son isn't as neat', says J. P. 'But if

PREVIOUS PAGES: The grocery and bar sections run along opposing walls, separated by a flagstone floor salvaged from the pavement of Dublin's Mountjoy Square.

you look at that, you'll see there was no messing with Larry.' The ledgers chronicle every transaction made in the pub from linseed oil and hydrated lime to legs of lamb and bottles of stout. The 1945 ledger shows how the Mayo farmers not only sheared their sheep twice in twelve months but also made more money on the second batch. The wool was dispatched to London and used as stuffing for bulletproof jackets. What makes Leonard's particularly interesting is that, unlike so many former shop-bars in Ireland, the pub still functions as a grocery and hardware store. The shelves are not simply stocked for the aesthetic benefit of tourists, but carry vital household items, cosmetic goods and food-stuffs. The salty bacon might no longer hang from the ceiling hooks but the slicer on the counter is still used daily to cut ham.

To the left of the pub, the old stores where Laurence kept his animal food, gas bottles and briquettes has been converted into a new wing, containing toilets and extra room to cater for the overspill from local wakes. Leonard's is a popular spot for funeral-goers because one of J. P.'s other careers is that of parish undertaker. J. P. has been dressing the corpses since he was a young man. The hearse, discreetly parked outside a funeral home to the right of his pub, is called out for business some forty times a year. A box beside the pub door lights up to notify passers-by of details as to precisely when the deceased is to be laid to rest. Being so in touch with the concept of death gives J. P. a zest for life. And, with Nephin Mor rising behind him, he stoutly maintains 'it's a lovely life'.

FACING PAGE AND ABOVE:
The exterior windows display a miscellany of washboards, buffer boards, wool-making appliances and advertisements for Brasso polish, Walnut Plug and Quaker Oats.

Brennan's (The Criterion)

BUNDORAN – CO. DONEGAL

Gleaming mirrors, brass cartridges and stuffed birds reach the ceiling

NAN AND PATRICIA BRENNAN WERE BORN in a bedroom above the bar that their grandparents opened on St Patrick's Day, 1900. The sisters have lived here all their lives, taking it in turns to serve from behind the pitch pine counter. Their grandparents called the pub 'The Criterion', after the noun meaning 'a standard by which something can be judged'. Genuine traditional bars are hard to find in 21st-century Donegal but The Criterion can certainly be judged as one of the few premises unsullied by the advent of modern times. 'This is my sort of pub', concurs an elderly Cork holiday-maker, supping on a stout. 'It's one of the few places where you can have a conversation and hear yourself think.'

Nan and Patricia started working here after they left school. 'When we were small we were always in and out and running about', recalls Nan. In 1947, the sisters helped their parents give the bar the robust overhaul which dictates its present-day interior. Classic chairs and sturdy tables made by Arnotts of Dublin meander gracefully over a cheerful Navan carpet into the deliciously wallpapered parlour and lounge area. Everything is immaculate, traditional, unfussy, simply inviting customers to take time out from the seasonal mayhem of the streets outside.

A dozen stools run along the wooden bar counter, behind which a pair of thirty-gallon Jameson barrels are set into the wall. Patricia indicates the brass mixers and hydrometers used to water the whiskey down so it was acceptable to the Customs officers; 'I could do it with my eyes closed', she laughs. Shelves rise

RIGHT: *A shelf laden with soda siphons, biscuit tins and antique bottles runs above one of the seating areas. To the left of a painting of Noah's Art, the original chimney has been converted into a clothes press. The original pine wainscoting is echoed in the butterscotch bench and stool.*

to ceiling height, stacked with well-polished glasses, rare bottles of whiskey, soda siphons, gleaming mirrors, brass cartridges, copperware and stuffed birds. Patrons rest their feet on a brass pole formerly located outside the pub for tying up horses. On the back wall, an aerial view of the verdant island of Inishmurray depicts the weather-battered rubble of a monastic settlement destroyed by Vikings 1,200 years ago.

Built in 1823, The Criterion began as a guesthouse for the growing number of well-to-do families arriving in 'Breezy Bundoran' to investigate just why the culture-loving Earl of Enniskillen had built his summer residence here on these raggedy Atlantic shores. By the time the Great Northern Railway arrived in 1866, the lively seaside resort was hailed as the Brighton of Ireland.

As with so many Irish towns, the ambience went downhill when the railway departed in 1957. The marching bands ceased marching and the gorgeous red and green train station was felled. By the early 1980s, the town had regained some of its gung-ho prosperity, aided by a bright neon amusement strip. But, for many, Brennan's is a delightful original, frozen in time.

The parlour and lounge were substantially refurbished after the Second World War, with the laying of a Navan carpet and the addition of these sturdy chairs, made by Arnotts of Dublin.

H. McGinn

This charming small pub is a mine of tall stories and banter

LEFT: *One of two special malt barrels purchased from Edmunds of Dublin in 1912.*

IN THE DEAD OF NIGHT, THE BUTLER MADE his way to the graveyard, eased open the vault door and struck a match to light his paraffin lamp. The coffin lay exactly where it had been placed two days earlier. He set the lamp down, crossed to the casket and slowly lifted the lid. Grasping the woman's hand, he began to remove the bejewelled rings. A large ruby ring, visible in the flickering light, resisted his strength. The butler produced a small penknife from his top pocket, inhaled deeply and set to work on the finger. The woman awoke and, in considerable pain, screamed loudly. The butler bolted into a nearby forest and was never seen again. The woman stepped out of the coffin, relocated her family and lived eerily ever after.

Such are the tales one is likely to hear when taking a drink in Annie McGinn's pub in Newbliss. The story has gained currency over the years and is now part of local folklore. The woman is supposed to have been one of the Murray-Kerrs who lived on one of the big estates outside Newbliss.

The pub was purchased in 1912 in trust for Annie's father, Hugh McGinn, by his cousin Phil McGinn. Hugh was in America at the time, having emigrated there with the rest of the family, the McGinns of Rockcorry. His time in America served him well and he mastered the bar trade, running a pub in downtown Manhattan with his brothers.

Soon after his return to Ireland, Hugh married Bridget Smith and settled down to run the grocery-bar formerly owned by the Manley family. Two special malt barrels he purchased from Edmunds of Dublin in 1912 rest above the bar to this day.

FACING PAGE: *Annie McGinn has lived and worked in the family pub in Monaghan all her life.*

Simple stools and chairs, blue and white tiles, DWD whiskey mirrors and advertisements for Guinness and Jameson provide a stark but intimate ambience.

The population of Newbliss in 1912 was about three hundred. The Rev. Joseph Gaston of Drumkeen was the only person who owned a 'mechanically-propelled vehicle', a powerful motorcycle with which he was known to harrow a crop of oats in his glebe-lands. To the back of the pub was a forge where a nailer was based; he slept in a loft above the forge.

The pub sits on the brow of a hill adjacent to the crumbling remains of a barracks built for the Royal Irish Constabulary in the early Victorian age. Shortly before Annie's birth in 1922, the barracks were occupied by the notorious Black and Tans, dispatched from Britain to suppress Irish rebels during the War of Independence. Annie recalls her mother's accounts of these troubled times when the barracks were constantly active with noisy drunks being confined to the lock-up and the coming and going of the soldiers in their Crossley tenders.

'She was a great woman', says Annie of her mother. 'A determined woman who would not brook any untoward behaviour or foul language in her pub.' Bridget died aged ninety-two in 1973, some ten years after her husband passed away at the equally respectable age of ninety-three. Annie and her brother Michael then took over the running of the premises. Michael has also since passed away.

Annie has left the pub as it was in her parents' day: small, warm, simply decorated. The only change has been the opening hours. 'I used to be open from half ten every day because there'd always be somebody. It was often someone just popping in for a bottle of porter after they'd gone to the creamery with milk.' The village was considerably busier before the railway, a lifeline for trade, closed in 1957. 'Those were the days! My old customers are all dead and gone. It's all young people now but we don't get many young people in here.'

Among her more intriguing customers are the miscellaneous artists, writers, musicians and other oddities attending nearby Annaghmakerrig, the retreat set up by the late theatre director Sir Tyrone Guthrie. Annie has served plenty of stout to such residents, often when they have literally just completed their magnum opus. She recalls Guthrie, a tall man, appearing in the doorway one Sunday morning when she and her mother had just returned from Mass. He was in pursuit of a bottle of whiskey for friends. 'Of course', replied Annie. 'He came right in after me, right behind the counter and put his hand way to the top shelf and took the bottle down.' Guthrie's noble attempt to boost the local economy by establishing a jam factory sadly collapsed – among other problems was a malfunctioning machine that failed to screw the jar lids on tightly enough.

Annie is a contented soul in her diminutive village pub. She still retains her custom, small though it may be. She is never happier than when there is a line of characters seated along the bar and the banter is in full flow.

McGinn's pub was bought in trust for Annie's father, Hugh McGinn, nearly a hundred years ago.

Gartlan's

Some of the regulars here have been coming for almost a century

'YOU'VE BEEN SITTING THERE SINCE MY grandfather's time', says Paul Gartlan.

'Aye, we've been coming here a long time', concurs seventy-year-old Dick Cassidy.

'Once a day, regular as clockwork, eh?' adds Johnny Browne.

'But not as long as old Paki Gargan', points out Dick.

'Paki was brought in here the day he was christened', explains Paul. 'And he drank here till he died aged ninety-four. He put nearly a century into the place.'

Gartlan's is a traditional grocery-bar, nicknamed the Hypermarket by its regulars. It has hardly changed since Paul's grandfather, George Gartlan, first opened it in 1911. 'Well, we've dusted it once or twice', admits Paul. The doorbell jingles as you enter, prompting those seated at the bar to about turn and give you the once over. To the left, the shop occupies an open-sided room, its tightly packed shelves stocked with Brillo Pads, tissues, Barry's tea, sugar, sardines and other non-perishables. Newcomers tend to drift down to the kitchen chairs and foot stools in a sitting area to the left. This is where musicians assemble on occasion, their feet tapping on the old tile floor, their pints balanced on window ledges between a Regentone long-wave radio, a kettle, an oil lamp. Pretty flowers clamber from small reed baskets hung from sash windows. The back wall is lined with poems and ballads etched by local literati, immortalizing wonderful nights. Photos of the local Muff Fair hang alongside a wheel from a 'Tin Lizzie', the first Ford Model T car that came to Ireland, and a collage entitled 'Paul has that Special Effect' depicting ten customers in various stages of self-induced stupor. People can watch television in another, smaller room at the back of the building.

George Gartlan and his brother John already ran a pub in Bailieborough called The Cusack Stand but George needed to diversify. Hence, the acquisition of the lease on this 17th-century thatched cottage in Kingscourt. George's wife, Rose Marie Mulvanny, came from Carnaross in Co. Meath and helped manage the business over the next four decades. Their four children were born in the building and were taught how to bottle beer and clean pipes from an early age. When George Gartlan died in 1946, his fifteen-year-old son Jim succeeded. Jim ran it for sixty-three years until his death aged seventy-six in 2007, when the business passed to Paul, the eldest of Jim's three sons.

FACING PAGE: *Owner Paul Gartlan and Gartlan's regular Eamon O'Reilly.*

Gartlan's has been in the same family for nearly a hundred years. Sharon Sheenan's son Brian is a practised hand at pitch and toss.

'And look at the shower of hoors I ended up with', chuckles Paul. 'In all honesty, I could have committed murder and got a lighter sentence. If you had a view from this side of the bar, believe me, it'd scare you.' Like his grandfather before him, Paul is a big man with an easy laugh. Like his father before him, the 44-year-old was born in the pub. He recalls helping his grandmother bottle beer as a toddler. 'You'll get your mineral when you've drunk your bottle of stout', she'd say. 'I pulled my first pint when I was six and I drank my first when I was five.' At the age of seven, Paul drank two fresh bottles 'and I had to be carried out of the house'.

'They used to call me Noddy at school', he says. 'At roll call, they'd say "Gartland" and spell it out. I'd say "No D" and so they called me Noddy.' Before he returned to Ireland, Paul worked on building sites in London and Germany. Back in the pub, his father was the absolute boss. 'Until he died, I was like a mushroom. Kept in the dark and covered in shite. When the whole lot was left in my lap, I was lost and, if it wasn't for that woman over there, I'd still be lost.' The woman he points to is his better half, Sharon Sheenan.

The shelves behind the bar are stacked to the ceiling with bric-a-brac from another age. There's an element of the fantastical – horns for summoning princely chariots, gourds for poisoning step-daughters, padlock keys for giant treasure chests. There's also plenty to baffle future generations: a savage-looking mole-trap from America; a hook for unbuckling carriages at the now abandoned Kingscourt railway station; a tobacco knife for cutting the plug; a powder-horn for measuring cartridge strength.

In the 1940s, George Gartlan purchased a field and quarry south-west of Kingscourt by Muff Rock. This is where one of Ireland's oldest traditional fairs takes place every August. The Muff Fair is considered an unofficial bank holiday for everyone in South Monaghan and the adjoining counties of Meath and Cavan. Farmers and traders from all parishes assemble with their Connemara ponies, Arab stallions, raggedy cobs and nimble-footed donkeys. Boy scouts strut purposefully down roads that echo with the sound of hand-slapping deals. Jim Gartlan was one of the key players behind the fair for over fifty years. His payback comes every year in the shape of a large corrugated barn, converted into a licensed pub and dance hall for the afternoon, where all the fairgoers gather to celebrate the magic of Muff. As well as music, there are keenly fought battles of pitch and toss and a rudimentary version of skittles which involves hurling a stick at the pins. The barn is owned and operated by the Gartlans. 'You wouldn't want an early start next morning after the Muff Fair', counsels local grain trader Richard Pringle.

Gartlan's is a pub with hearty conversation at its core. Whiskery men in Tommy Makem jumpers wheeze with laughter at each other's wisecracks. Their fathers were men who walked amid cabbages and potatoes with horse, cart and whitethorn stick.

Kingscourt's history dates to those dark days when Ireland was perpetually at war with invaders and with itself. The town was named after the defeated King James II spent two nights in nearby Cabra Castle on his retreat from the Battle of the Boyne. Today, the busy market town is home to the main production plant of Gypsum Industries and is the headquarters of the Kingspan Group, one of Ireland's most powerful building suppliers. There are so many newcomers in town that old timers are unsure whether to greet the people they pass on the pavements. 'It's gone up a bit in the world since I left it', says Dick, a recently returned émigré. 'There was one time it was a very poor part of the country. Now everyone's building big houses for three or four hundred thousand euros.'

At times such as these, it is important to have a publican who takes his role seriously. Paul Gartlan makes his visitors feel wanted. He provides them with good drink and considerable humour and, with Sharon beside him, he is to be commended for maintaining the very essence of a traditional Irish pub.

Whiskey casks and beer barrels double as drinks tables to one side of the grocery.

Contemporary Heritage

The length and breadth of Ireland the most savvy pub owners are swimming against the tide of commercialization and homogenization. Banishing the television and loud music, they are returning to the pub's roots, catering for a growing band of connoisseurs who know exactly what they are looking for. The four new-generation bars discussed here are quintessentially Irish, yet with a twist that inspires faith in the future of the trade. They combine the best aspects of the traditional pub — the décor, the charm, the enveloping ambience — with the crisper lines of the 21st century, and are, we hope, the future of the Irish pub.

The Sky & the Ground, Wexford.

The Sky & the Ground

WEXFORD – CO. WEXFORD

Most pub spies would be hard pushed to identify this as a 1996 creation

Blackboards invite passers-by to sample
the food, drink and music offered
within. The pub sign was designed
by Martin Hopkins.

IN 1995, JOHNNIE BARRON and his wife, Nuala, entered the townhouse where
his widowed great-aunt had lived. Known as The Glen, the building was slowly
collapsing, its timber walls riddled with holes as though it had been the setting for
some unbridled Wild West gunfight. As they walked through the rooms, Johnnie's
eyes ran over the wainscoting and floorboards that had held firm, the stained-glass
windows that had somehow escaped the damage. When the Barrons attempted
to enter one room, they found the door would not open. A screwdriver was
summoned and the hinges removed. Piled high in front of the door was a mountain
of magazines. Their late great-aunt, Kathleen Molloy, had been a travel writer for
the *Irish Times* during the 1930s. The postman had known her well, delivering
package after package of advertising brochures and magazines from publicity-
seeking tourism organizations across the globe. She kept every one of them.

In his twenties, Johnnie Barron went from Ireland to Wales four times a day
looking after the duty-free section on the Rosslare to Fishguard ferry. One of the
downsides of becoming part of the European Union was the abolition of duty free.
With Johnnie in danger of being out of work, he and Nuala began to consider their

FACING PAGE: *Old-style frosted-glass
doors and vintage tin tobacco and cocoa
advertisements form the main entrance.*

Pages from early 20th-century travel and fashion magazines are housed in ecclesiastical frames and pepper walls throughout the pub.

options. 'We took a fancy to open a pub', he says. The Barrons were to be the first publicans in either family. Johnnie's forbears came from the coast near Tramore and descended from the Barrons of Burnchurch, Co. Kilkenny. Nuala's family, the Beavers, came from England. Both had grandfathers who had worked in foundries – Johnnie's outside Waterford, Nuala's in Wexford.

In 1995, they purchased The Kingdom Bar at the south end of the old Norman port town of Wexford. It had been a pub since at least the 1890s (when licensed to a James Cullimore) and was sited in a part of town reclaimed from swamps by enterprising Victorian engineers.

The Kingdom Bar had burned down two years earlier and lay derelict. Inspired by the work done on Geoff's in Waterford City (see pp. 176–9), Johnnie and Nuala took it down and, incorporating a former butcher's shop next door, built a brand new one in its place. 'I wanted a pub that had soul and atmosphere', he explained. It is a considerable achievement that the Barrons have created a pub, full of soul, that even the most seasoned pub spies would be hard pushed to identify as a 1996 creation.

One enters into a room that smells of the old world and seems to go on forever. There is nothing but dark wood, dim lights, vintage advertisements and rickety shelves groaning with curiosities. Much of this effect had been achieved through his great-aunt Kathleen's legacy. Johnnie salvaged the wainscoting, floorboards and stained glass from her house and placed it with meticulous precision along the walls and floors of his pub. He went through her vast collection of magazines (at least, the ones that hadn't been destroyed by damp), and found some eighty old-style advertisements that were appealing. He visited a church auction where large bundles of holy pictures, each one framed, were being sold as a job lot. The chosen advertisements were duly framed and hung along the wooden panelling.

A red bench to the left leads around to a small snug of anaglypta wallpaper decorated with bookmakers' memorabilia and photographs of four generations of Barron forbears. A large poster for DWD whiskey points to the atmospheric Heavens Above restaurant upstairs. A piano, manufacturer unknown, marks the entrance to the main bar. Chipped enamel lampshades hang low over a counter, salvaged from Gaynor's shoe shop, now capped by three discreetly assertive tap banks. London signwriter Martin Hopkins crafted the old-style signs above shelves salvaged from an old chemist shop and fitted by Wexford carpenter Dennis Frayne. The shelves are now stuffed with Sunlight soaps, Jeyes flats and other 'where are they now?' household names. 'I don't deliberately go out and try to buy stuff', insists Johnnie. 'It's just whatever comes to me.'

A saloon-style partition points to a brick wall in the far distance, hung with an old geographical map of Ireland. To the right, a marble fireplace dated 1864 heats a series of private wainscoted enclaves, each one furnished with marble tables, games

tables, stained-glass panes and classic advertisements for Chivas Regal, Wills Gold Flake, Donard Dew Old Irish Whiskey, Tayto Crisps and other goods that promise 'sweet harmony'. Few chairs match. The floorboards in this part came from an old malting house in Birmingham.

The stained-glass panes on this partition were salvaged from a derelict family home.

The Sky & the Ground is a musical pub with a singer-songwriter club on Tuesdays and traditional music on Mondays and Wednesdays. Among those who play regularly is 86-year-old fiddler Gerry Forde, who, old-timers take heart, started the regular Monday night sessions when he was seventy-five. The pub's name came from the title of an album released by another Wexford musician, Pierce Turner, a relation of Nuala's, memorably described by *Hot Press* as 'Joyce with a voice, Yeats on skates'.

'We get a very mixed crowd' says Johnnie. 'Eighteen to ninety, right across the board.' He appreciates that a pub must make money to survive. He leases the restaurant upstairs and has landscaped a fine beer garden to the rear. Perhaps most importantly he has converted the former butcher's shop into a sports bar, the solitary room with a television. 'We built this pub so people could have a chat but if the lads want to watch sport, they can go in there.' Whether Johnnie's children choose to get involved in the business remains to be seen but the very fact that he has ensured the pub is proactive will certainly ignite their passions. All too often, it is where parents seem to be doing nothing to stay afloat that their children baulk and run. The Sky & the Ground is an excellent example of how to do something and how to do it right.

Tayto are credited with having developed cheese and onion crisps in 1954.

Geoff's

You half expect a press-gang to slip in to heave your body onto a man-of-war

'THE DEVIL IN THE CORNER' WAS HOW one publican described the television in his bar. 'I took it away one time and they all gave out to me.' The simple fact, we are told, is that 21st-century drinkers need the visual stimulation of a television in order to enjoy the whole pub experience. It does not necessarily matter if the volume is on. Indeed, many pubs choose to have a radio relaying completely different information to that suggested by the flickering plasma screens above the bar. Few can doubt that televisions destroy the ambience of a pub. Yes, there are certain sporting occasions

Reassuring proverbs are framed upon the walls.

when such destruction might be merited. But such occasions must be occasional. They cannot dominate. In all too many instances, the hypnotic screens remain defiantly on, day and night, seriously hampering any chance of creative conversation by the poor souls perched along the bar.

There are those who argue that showing matches on television brings in the money. That may be. But those who want to make money by less perfidious means would be well advised to look at Geoff's in Waterford. This family-owned pub is the most successful in the city. At weekends, queues form outside its doors. The pub can accommodate 750 people at maximum capacity. By day the pub doubles as a café and wholesome meals are served through until the evening. And there is not one television in the three-storey building.

The reason Geoff's is so popular is probably because its eponymous owner has been so successful at maintaining the essence of the grocery-bar which his grandfather, Geoffrey Power, founded here on this site over a century ago. Back in 1906, the pub's location was just about perfect. Every day, crowds congregated in the Apple Market just outside its front door. Less than two hundred metres away was the stand where all the jarvey cars gathered to collect and deliver passengers from the city's hinterland. The British Army stationed a garrison in the nearby barracks.

Right through until the 1960s, the pub could count on a high quota of farmers to occupy the counter stools. Geoff's mother, Eleanor, recalls how they would arrive in from the countryside, park their carts around the Apple Market clock, and present her husband, Michael, with a list of their desired goods. They would then sit down and have a drink or two while their groceries were boxed and loaded up onto their carts. By early evening, the sing-songs were in full flow. It wasn't just farmers either. One of the regulars was Major Redmond Cunningham, MC, a veteran of the Arnhem campaign who frequently met his friends in the bar to play cards.

By the time Michael Power passed away in 1977, much of Waterford's lifeblood had moved away from John Street towards the Quays. The Apple Market had largely

dried up and the farmers now did their shopping in supermarkets. However, hope returned that same year when Michael's second son, Geoff, returned from Dublin to take stock of the situation. His plan was to stay in Waterford for a year and then move on. He has been there ever since.

One of Geoff's first steps was to remove the Formica counter tops, beauty boards and black and white Dunlop tiles, thus returning the bar to its original timber and

A wide red-tiled floor leads to the back bar area, bedecked with railing, panelling and old frosted windows salvaged from local schools, hotels and shops.

slate finish. He also evicted the dartboard and the television. In time, he extended the bar into the grocery section. And for the next three decades he and his team set about converting the bar into its present incarnation, simultaneously breathing new life into this part of town.

Somehow, despite the enormity of the space and the hotch-potch nature of its furnishings, Geoff's still feels like a genuine old-world bar. You could imagine a press-gang slipping in to heave your drunken body onto a man-of-war. One enters past the original etched-glass sign into a vast emporium of dark woods, slate floors, a veritable orgy of sofas, tables and chairs veiled beneath ecclesiastical partitions, peeking through balustrade railings, sprawling merrily up spiral stairwells. Every fitting, from floorboards to the innermost reveals, seems to be different. In the main drinking area to the back right are tables of every shape and size. Long rectangles. Big squares. Small circles. Wide ovals. One table, known as 'The United Nations', can seat fourteen. Seating is likewise an assortment of sticklebacks, long benches, church pews, sturdy armchairs and slick stroll-back dining chairs. Walls are decked with gilded mirrors, classic advertisements, stitchwork quotations, bawdy prints, photographs of Powers family members from earlier generations, a Robert Ballagh Campbell Soups print, a magnificent billboard poster for 1992's sun-drenched Fleadh Mór Tramore festival.

Shelves and dressers appear at unexpected moments, laden with vintage

ports, ledger books, headless statues and memorabilia of the Waterford Instrumental Society. The bar counter, its timbers salvaged from an old bank, occupies a square at the centre of the premises. Indeed, most of the furniture has been salvaged – banisters from the old Grenville Hotel, panels from the Bartons' quayside merchant house, signs from nearby draperies and outfitters that have since closed, Douglas fir floorboards from a mill in Graiguenamanagh, chunky slate flags from an old pub in Portlaw upon which roughshod tanners once stood.

Not everything is as it seems. Tony Cullen, the chief carpenter, taps a splendidly ornate Elizabethan arch above him and whispers the word 'Medite' – a type of MDF. 'I've often felt most good design comes from accidents', he confides. Tony is a part-time set designer for Waterford's Red Kettle Theatre Company. As such he has learned not only how to work to limited budgets, but also how to trick the passing eye. Many 'antiques' scattered through the pub were created for a performance of Arthur Miller's *The Price*. Tony's theatrical bent reaches its apex in the latest extension, added in 2005, incorporating part of an old laneway running directly beneath the old city wall.

Geoff's is a large pub, comprised of the original grocery-bar, an old bookshop, a small printing factory, a medieval laneway and a backyard. It's likely Geoff will continue to expand his empire in coming years. As his mother, Eleanor, says, 'he has the business'. 'It's an ongoing project', concurs Tony. 'Which means we're never going to finish. The plans will be drawn when the job is done.'

A large dining table made of Douglas fir is nicknamed 'The United Nations' as people from all walks of life fill the fourteen chairs around it night after night.

FACING PAGE: *The original etched-glass Groceries and Spirits sign near the entrance is a reminder that this was once a grocery-bar.*

De Barra's

Even the bar staff are all gifted musicians

EVERYONE NEEDS A LITTLE SHAKE AROUND every now and then. It's good for the soul to be tipped upside down and given an unexpected makeover. De Barra's pub in the pretty West Cork town of Clonakilty is a classic example. A hundred years ago, this was a straightforward grocery-bar with a bakery and storehouse to the rear. The Republican leader Michael Collins probably nipped in for a loaf of bread back when he was a young lad living locally. Fast forward to 1974 when Eileen Barry, the daughter of the house, married a heavyweight boxer from Portlaoise and the whole show went leftfield.

Bobby Blackwell became a boxer because his father had been a boxer before him. Indeed, his father had managed the Irish boxing team during the 1940s when it counted among its ranks such golden-gloved greats as Johnny Caldwell, Harry Perry

The wall above the fireplace is hung with instruments given to the owner by past customers, including a saxophone that belonged to Manfred Mann and some uilleann pipes played at the Chicago World's Fair in 1893.

and Fred Teele. Bobby hung up his boxing gloves in 1975, had a stint at plumbing and moved to Clonakilty in 1980 to see what he could do with his in-laws' pub. 'It was just a country pub until Bobby introduced the music', says Eileen. Bobby has always loved music and he passionately believed that music would be the saving grace of the pub. Twenty-seven years later, you would be hard pressed to find a venue in Ireland with a more genuine enthusiasm for first-rate music than the de Barra's Folk Club. 'There's Carnegie Hall, The Royal Albert, Sydney Opera House – and then there's de Barra's', said Christy Moore. Christy is one of many well-known musicians who found the mellow, unassuming ambience of de Barra's perfectly suited to their ambitions.

The instant one enters the pub, the musical ambience takes over. The wall, stage left, is covered in flutes, fiddles, bodhráns, pipes and saxophones. Unlike most rock cafes, these instruments have a very real history. The uilleann pipes were played by a Tullamore piper at the Chicago World's Fair in 1893. The mandolin criss-crossed Ireland for four years with Paddy Keenan and The Bothy Band. The fender jazz bass guitar belonged to the late Noel Redding, the former Jimi Hendrix bassist and a celebrated resident of Clonakilty. Redding also presented Bobby with the gleaming double platinum record of *Are You Experienced*, the psychedelic debut album by The Jimi Hendrix Experience.

Wherever possible, Bobby and Eileen have left the original pub interior intact. That includes the scuffed red floor, laid down by Polish workers during the Second World War, and apparently made from sawdust and mangle beet held together by blood from an abbatoir. They have also left the original bar in place, complete with a small snug. The most dominant features of the snug are the front-page newspaper accounts of the sinking of the *Lusitania*, a British luxury ocean liner, by a German U-boat in 1915. Among the 1,198 people who died in the attack were 128 Americans,

A cascade of flower baskets ensures de Barra's helps maintain Clonakilty's reputation as one of the neatest and most cheerful towns in Ireland.

and the outrage felt in the United States played a part in bringing that country into the First World War. Bobby recalled an occasion when two Americans were reading these words. An old man seated beside them coughed slightly and said quietly, 'I'm a survivor'. 'My God', said the Americans. They bought him brandy and stout for the remainder of the day while he talked cryptically of life on the *Lusitania*. When the Americans left, Bobby went up to the man and said, 'Con, you were never on the *Lusitania* in your life'. 'I never said I was', replied the 96-year-old Clonakilty postman. 'I just said "I'm a survivor". And I am a fecking survivor.'

The corridor to the de Barra Folk Club is lined with classic advertising posters and a platinum record presented by Noel Redding.

The bar runs through into the old kitchen where Eileen's family had breakfast in her youth; the stove is still in position. A staircase to the left is bedecked with colourful masks, one carved with a chainsaw. A dark wooden corridor lined with photographs, bawdy cartoons and advertising posters leads directly to the purpose-built auditorium where the de Barra Folk Club now congregates on musical evenings. The audience sit on old church benches and sewing-machine tables with school desk counters. A large gap in the ceiling, which Christy Moore refers to as 'Bobby's Hole', enables another whole floor to listen in.

If the bar staff appear to be particularly interested in the tunes, that's because they're all gifted musicians in their own right. For instance, singer-songwriter Gavin Moore frequently serves pints here between his grand tours of Europe. On Wednesday nights, the stage is 'dressed up' as a sitting room for a particularly beautiful evening of quasi-theatrical entertainment.

The line up changes all the time and, with its traditional roots, there have sometimes been as many as twenty musicians playing at once. The only instrument Bobby Blackwell plays is the till. And he plays it well. But he has been careful to ensure the venue does not get too big for its boots.

Bobby is the perfect host. His bashful twinkling eyes, 'Old Man of the Sea' beard and boxer's physique contain a spirit much given to humour, storytelling and music. His attitude to de Barra's has been simultaneously clever and proactive. He has retained the essence of the original, while simultaneously serving hot lunches and hosting some of the most atmospheric music nights in the land. It comes as no surprise that Bobby and Eileen's son Raymond is now one of the key players in the family business.

Masks presented to the owner by customers rise up a stairwell. An antique coffee grinder is perched on an old sewing table. A British Army recruitment poster exudes gentle satire.

Gertie Browne

ATHLONE – CO. WESTMEATH

Vintage adverts and brass lamps recreate the charm of an old-world pub

RUNNING OVER TWO HUNDRED MILES FROM its source to the sea, the Shannon is the longest river in Europe west of the Loire. The town of Athlone lies about halfway down and has been expanding ever since smart-thinking Normans threw a bridge across the river here in the 12th century. In June 1691, the town was the setting for a crucial showdown when William of Orange's army of 25,000 soldiers pitched their cannon along the eastern riverbanks, aimed them at the town and unleashed mayhem. Athlone's besieged citizens valiantly strove to prevent the enemy crossing the bridge but, when the Williamites identified another fordable point just downriver, it was all over. On 30 June, the Williamites crossed the Shannon and took possession of the town.

'Do you think this might be from the battle?', asks Michael Loughman, holding up a decrepit musket salvaged from the Shannon close to his pub. It's certainly a possibility. The streetscape where Gertie Browne stands is named Custume Place after an Irish dragoon sergeant who led ten men on a suicidal mission across the river to disrupt the siege. Surely the riverbed that divides Athlone must be full of bits and pieces that once belonged to Custume and the countless others who also died during those eleven bloody days.

Michael believes a thirsty soldier from 1691 might have struck lucky with a tankard of ale right here on the site he purchased fifteen years ago. In fact, he'd wager there's been some class of drinking den here since the Normans arrived. For all that, he would struggle to beat Sean's Bar across the river which, crowned 'Ireland's oldest pub' by the *Guinness Book of Records*, claims to have been serving passing pilgrims since the early 10th century.

Michael Loughman was born in West Tipperary in 1948. His father, an electrician, moved the family to Athlone in the 1950s when he was employed to work on the Rural Electrification Scheme in Westmeath. Like his mother before him, Michael opted for a teaching career, focusing on maths and technical drawing. From 1969 onwards, he spent his summers working as a bartender in New York's Upper East Side. By 1993, Michael and his wife, Mary, also a New York veteran, had earned sufficient money to buy a pub of their own.

FACING PAGE: *A knight in shining armour, purchased in New York, stands guard above family patriarch Sergeant Dinny Cunnaire, Irish Army, retired.*

Portraits and vintage maps overlook an alcove by the stairs. A timber Jameson cask serves as a table.

Named for a former owner, a pub has stood on the site of Gertie Browne since at least the 17th century.

Before the Loughmans purchased the three-storey Georgian building in Athlone, the pub was called 'The Hooker Bar', after the traditional sailing boats found in Galway. From 1905 until the 1950s, the pub belonged to the Browne family, one of Athlone's great boat-building firms. The Brownes specialized in sailing craft and lake boats, and had a long association with the Lough Ree Yacht Club. An advertisement in an Athlone Guide from 1896 reads: 'Michael Browne, Fisherman, The Strand, Athlone – Yachts, Mermaids, Thames Skiffs & other Craft for Sale & Hire'. As licensed salmon fishermen, the Brownes could legally net salmon at some of the 'salmon draws' in Athlone. On the death of Frank Browne senior, the business passed to his son Teddy, the last of the boat-builders and a cousin of the American novelist James T. Farrell, author of the *Studs Lonigan* trilogy. Teddy's wife, Gertie, was a formidable woman more than capable of subduing any customers who got out of hand. After his death, she continued to run the bar and shop for some years before selling to Joe O'Meara of Connaught Street. 'Gertie would sit up at the top window', says Michael. 'When she moved, the whole place went silent.' The name 'Gertie Browne' appealed to Michael so much that he named the pub in her honour. The 'R' in the name 'Gertie' is reversed on the sign. 'Sure I put the "o" upside down and nobody says anything about it', mutters Michael.

Gertie Browne is the sort of Irish pub you'd expect to find in New York. It's certainly got all the right traits – tongue-and-groove walls, pitch pine counters, rattly windows bulging with old box cameras and soda siphons and framed by raggedy curtains, original posters for Keegan's Irish Whiskey and nipple ointment, shelves rising up walls and framed pages from, of all newspapers, the *New York Herald*. As it happens, the Loughmans recreated pretty much everything from top to bottom. Athlone carpenter Mick Casserly designed the telephone box and the grocery drawers, but most of the timberwork has been salvaged. The bar's timber came from a convent in Moate. The tongue-and-groove panelling came from the town's Victorian military barracks; in certain places, they are replicated by cutting recessed four-panel doors in two. Church furniture is reincarnated as benches, while the heat from a Congress stove rebounds off whiskey barrels and a sprightly piano.

The decoration is genuine, personal and, above all, Athlone. A room to the side is named for John Count McCormack, the world-famous tenor born in the town in 1884.

The walls are decorated with his records and songsheets, memorabilia from his life and photographs of the Athlone Woollen Mills where his parents worked. Bleached steer heads, po-faced gargoyles and images of the Connaught Rangers preparing for action in the Zulu campaigns are reflected in bright brassy lamps. Bills for the long-gone Ritz cinema hang alongside photographs of Michael's late father and other drinking comrades past. A photograph of the *Titanic* hangs in tribute to Margaret Rice, a housekeeper from Athlone, who perished in the tragedy along with all five of her sons. But there is humour here to, such as a map depicting the Athlone Underground.

Mary Loughman was keen to serve food but her husband refused to countenance the presence of salt and pepper cellars in the bar. A compromise was reached when they expanded their operation to incorporate the 'Hatters Lane' restaurant in a separate part of the building. The name of this successful Hollywood theme restaurant recalls the milliners who used to operate from here. For sure, concedes Michael, 'the restaurant brings in the business'. Michael believes that, while Irish pubs are going through a major transition at the present, it is simply a thinning out process that will level off in due course. 'But maybe it won't be so long before the government are giving out grants to people who want to open a pub.'

A large sign above an archway recalls the nickname of a small man-made harbour created in Athlone as part of an 1820s 'relief scheme'. The labourers were paid in 'stirabout' (porridge).

Atlantic Ocean

Celtic Sea

Saint George's Channel

Irish Sea

BUSHMILLS
⑱ BALLYCASTLE

Donegal

Londonderry

Antrim

Tyrone

Ulster

Lough Neagh

BELFAST ⑯ ⑰

⑮ PORTADOWN

Down

BUNDORAN ㉝

Fermanagh

GLASLOUGH ⑭ Armagh

Monaghan

Louth

CLONES ㉞
NEWBLISS

⑬ SLIGO

Sligo

Leitrim

Cavan

Mayo

LAHARDANE ㉜

Roscommon

Connacht

WESTPORT

Longford

KINGSCOURT ㉟

NAVAN ③

ROSCOMMON

FOUR ROADS ㉛

Westmeath

⑲ HILL OF SKRYNE

MAGHERA ㉚

Meath

Leinster

ATHLONE ㊴

Offaly

Dublin

① ② DUBLIN

Liffey

GALWAY ⑫

Galway

Aran Islands

Galway Bay

Kildare

BALLITORE

㉙ BALLYVAUGHAN

Laois

ATHY ⑳

Wicklow

㉑ GREENANE

④

⑤ ABBEYLEIX

Clare

CLOGH ㉔

Carlow

NEWTOWN

KILLKENNY ⑥

Kilkenny

② BORRIS

KILRUSH ⑪

㉖ CASTLECONNELL

Shannon

Tipperary

GLIN ㉗

㉘ BALLYLONGFORD

LISTOWEL

Limerick

Wexford

FETHARD ⑦

WEXFORD ㊱

Munster

Kerry

Lee

Waterford

CALLAGHANE

WATERFORD ㊲

⑨ ⑩ DINGLE

Dingle Bay

Cork

FERMOY

㉕

CORK

BANTRY

KINSALE ⑧

CLONAKILTY ㊳

Bantry Bay

1 ⊢━━━━━━━┤ 50 MILES
1 ⊢━━━━━━━┤ 80 KM

The number for each pub is shown on the map opposite.

Urban Retreat

1 The Long Hall
51 South Great George's Street
Dublin 2
Tel: +353 (0)1 475 1590

2 The Stag's Head
Dame Court
Dublin 2
Tel: +353 (0)1 671 3701
www.thestagshead.ie

3 Bermingham's
7 Ludlow Street
Navan
Co. Meath
Tel: +353 (0)46 902 9829

4 Clancy's
12 Leinster Street
Athy
Co. Kildare
Tel: +353 (0)59 863 1964

5 E. J. Morrissey's
Main Street
Abbeyleix
Co. Laois
Tel: +353 (0)57 873 1281

6 Lenehan's
10 Barrack Street
Kilkenny City
Co. Kilkenny
Tel: +353 (0)56 772 1621

7 McCarthy's
Main Street
Fethard
Co. Tipperary
Tel: +353 (0)52 31149
www.mccarthyshotel.net

8 The Bulman
Summercove
Kinsale
Co. Cork
Tel: +353 (0)21 477 2131
www.thebulman.com

9 Dick Mack's
Green Steet
Dingle
Co. Kerry
Tel: +353 (0)66 915 1960

10 J. Curran's
Main Street
Dingle
Co. Kerry
Tel: +353 (0)66 915 1110

11 Crotty's
Market Square
Kilrush
Co. Clare
Tel: +353 (0)65 905 2470
www.crottyspubkilrush.com

12 Tigh Neachtain's
17 Cross St
Galway City
Co. Galway
Tel: +353 (0)91 568820

13 Thomas Connolly's
Holborn Street and
Markievicz Street
Sligo
Co. Sligo
Tel: +353 (0)71 916 7377

14 J. & W. Wright's
Glaslough
Co. Monaghan
Tel: +353 (0)47 88106

15 McConville's
(The Mandeville Arms)
Mandeville Street
Portadown
Co. Armagh
BT62 3PD
Tel: +44 (0)28 3833 2070

16 Kelly's Cellars
30–32 Bank Street
Belfast
Co. Antrim
BT1 1HL
Tel: +44 (0)28 9024 6058

17 The Crown Liquor
Saloon
46 Great Victoria Street
Belfast
Co. Antrim
BT2 7BA
Tel: +44 (0)28 9027 9901
www.crownbar.com

18 House of McDonnell
Castle Street
Ballycastle
Co. Antrim
BT54 6TAS
Tel: +44 (0)28 2076 2975
www.houseofmcdonnell.com

Rural Charm

19 O'Connell's
Hill of Skryne
Co. Meath
Tel: +353 (0)46 902 5122

20 E. Butterfield's
(The Harp Bar)
Ballitore
Co. Kildare
Tel: +353 (0)59 862 3329

21 M. J. Byrne
Greenane
Co. Wicklow
Tel: +353 (0)40 446195

22 P. F. Smyth
Newtown
Co. Carlow
Tel: +353 (0)59 972 7159

23 M. O'Shea
Main Street
Borris
Co. Carlow
Tel: +353 (0)59 977 3106

24 Somers
Clogh
Co. Kilkenny
Tel: +353 (0)56 444 2133

25 Mary Kennedy's
Callaghane Bridge
Co. Waterford
Tel: +353 (0)51 382230

26 P. J. Guerin
(The Kingfisher)
Castleconnell
Co. Limerick
Tel: +353 (0)61 377407
www.ireland360.com/
kingfisher

27 O'Shaughnessy's
(The Ivy House)
Glin
Co. Limerick
Tel: +353 (0)68 34115

28 M. Finucane
Quay Street
Ballylongford
Co. Kerry
Tel: +353 (0)68 43243

29 O'Loclainn's Irish
Whiskey Bar
Ballyvaughan
Co. Clare
Tel: +353 (0)65 707 7006
www.irishwhiskeybar.com

30 Murray's
Maghera
Co. Westmeath
Tel: +353 (0)90 648 5345

31 Coyle & Sons
Four Roads
Mount Talbot
Co. Roscommon
Tel: +353 (0)90 662 3315

32 Leonard's
Lahardane
Ballina
Co. Mayo
Tel: +353 (0)96 51003

33 Brennan's
(The Criterion)
Main Street
Bundoran
Co. Donegal
Tel: +353 (0)71 984 1810

34 H. McGinn
Newbliss
Co. Monaghan
Tel: +353 (0)47 54450

35 Gartlan's
Lower Main Street
Kingscourt
Co. Cavan
Tel: +353 (0)42 966 7003

Contemporary Heritage

36 The Sky & the Ground
112 South Main Street
Wexford
Co. Wexford
Tel: +353 (0)53 912 1273

37 Geoff's
John Street
Waterford City
Co. Waterford
Tel: +353 (0)51 874787

38 De Barra's
55 Pearse Street
Clonakilty
Co. Cork
Tel: +353 (0)23 33381
www.debarra.ie

39 Gertie Browne
Custume Place
Athlone
Co. Westmeath
Tel: +353 (0)90 647 4848

During our Grand Tour of Ireland we stayed in a variety of places ranging from simple B&Bs to fairy-tale castles and 21st-century boutique hotels. Listed below is a selection of the highlights from our trip, commencing in Dublin and then moving clockwise around the island.

The Morgan Hotel
10 Fleet Street
Temple Bar
Dublin 2
Tel: +353 (0)1 643 7000
www.themorgan.com

Newgrange Hotel
Bridge Street
Navan
Co. Meath
Tel: +353 (0)46 907 4100
www.newgrangehotel.ie

Bellinter House
Navan
Co. Meath
Tel: +353 (0)46 903 0900
www.bellinterhouse.com

Hibernian Hotel
1 Ormonde Street
Kilkenny City
Co. Kilkenny
Tel: +353 (0)56 777 1888
www.kilkennyhibernianhotel.com

McCarthy's Hotel
Main Street
Fethard
Co. Tipperary
Tel: +353 (0)52 31149
www.mccarthyshotel.net

Arlington Lodge
John's Hill,
Waterford City
Co. Waterford
Tel: +353 (0)51 878584
www.arlingtonlodge.com

Ballyvolane House
Castlelyons
Fermoy
Co. Cork
Tel: +353 (0)25 36349
www.ballyvolanehouse.ie

The Blue Haven
Pearse Street
Kinsale
Co. Cork
Tel: +353 (0)21 477 2209
www.bluehavenkinsale.com

The Maritime Hotel
The Quay
Bantry
Co. Cork
Tel: +353 (0)27 54700
www.themaritime.ie

Doyle's Townhouse
John Street .
Dingle
Co. Kerry
Tel: +353 (0)66 91 5 1174
www.doylesofdingle.com

Listowel Arms Hotel
The Square
Listowel
Co. Kerry
Tel: +353 (0)68 21500
www.listowelarms.com

Glin Castle
Glin
Co. Limerick
Tel: +353 (0)68 34173
www.glincastle.com

Crotty's
Market Square
Kilrush
Co. Clare
Tel: +353 (0)65 905 2470
www.crottyspubkilrush.com

Gregan's Castle Hotel
Ballyvaughan
Co Clare
Tel: +353 (0)65 707 7005
www.gregans.ie

Forster Court Hotel
Forster Street
Galway City
Co. Galway
Tel: +353 (0)91 564111
www.forstercourthotel.com

Abbey Hotel
Galway Road
Roscommon
Co. Roscommon
Tel: +353 (0)90 662 6240
www.abbeyhotel.ie

Westport Plaza Hotel
Castlebar Street
Westport
Co. Mayo
Tel: +353 (0)98 51166
www.westportplazahotel.ie

The Glasshouse
Swan Point
Sligo
Co. Sligo
Tel: +353 (0)71 919 4300
www.theglasshouse.ie

Hilton Park
Clones
Co. Monaghan
Tel: +353 (0)47 56007
www.hiltonpark.ie

Castle Leslie
Glaslough
Co. Monaghan
Tel: +353 (0)47 88100
www.castleleslie.com

Ravenhill Guest House
690 Ravenhill Road
Belfast
Co. Antrim
BT6 0BZ
Tel: +44 (0)28 9020 7444
www.ravenhillguesthouse.com

The Bushmills Inn
9 Dunluce Road
Bushmills
Co. Antrim
BT57 8QG
Tel: +44 (0)28 2073 3000
www.bushmillsinn.com

ACKNOWLEDGMENTS

The number of people who have helped us has been truly astonishing. We would particularly like to thank the following: Our beautiful wives, Ally and Jo – for your patience and support; the publicans and bartenders of Ireland – for your time and refreshments; Thames & Hudson – for bringing this book into being.

Also, for directing us along the way: Aidan Barry, Rohan Boyle, Red Cabot, Simon Carswell, John & Ger Clancy, Paul Clements, Andrew Davidson, Se Merry Doyle, Matthew Durdin-Robertson, Nicky ffrench Davis, Mathew Forde, Finn Gillespie, Aine Grealy, Mary-Claire Grealy, Nicoleen Greer, Nicky Haslan, John Hayden, Shane Hegarty, George Hook, Jnr, Alannah Hopkin, Hugo & Roz Jellett, Rory Keating, Stephen Kelly and Margaret Scott of the Federation of the Licensed Retail Trade, Dave Kennedy, Eliz Lee, Gerry Lynch, Richard Morris of Janklow & Nesbit, Orla Nelligan, Hugh Oram, Denis O'Reilly, William Paterson, Michael Purcell, Conor Ryan, George Thomas, Conor Walsh and Nick Wilkinson.

PATRONS

We take a heartfelt bow to the following patrons of this book.
Arabella Annesley, Annie Barclay & Neil Burkey, John Barron, Emma Beurghs, Bobby Blackwell, Justin Bock, Grattan Boylan, John William Brady, Niall Brennan, Derek Briggs, Siobhan Buchanan Johnson, Andrew & Nicola Bunbury, Jemima Bunbury, Marco Buosí, Hugo Chittenden Esq., John Coffey, Michael Collins, Clodagh Conroy, Tim Coote, Nick Coveney, Crotty's Pub, The Crystal Bar (Beacon Hotel), Mark Cummings & Eimhear Lowry, Martin D'Alton, Henry De Bromhead, Paddy Deering, Terence & Bridget Dempsey, Kate & Simon Dick, Fiona Doherty, Trevor Edmond Dolan, David & Hannah Ross, Nick & Delia Drummond, Gavin Elliot, Ninian Falkiner, Joanna Fennell, William & Lesley Fennell, Paul Finnerty, Michael & Deirdre Finucane, Desmond FitzGerald, Knight of Glin, Donal Flanagan, Thomas Flanagan, Sarah Fletcher, Jonathan Forrest, Mathew Gallagher, Rachel Gamble, Tim & Courtney Garneau, P. J. Gibbons, Paddy Guerin, Rory Guinness, Trish Hawkey, Eduard Hemple, Marcus Houlihan, Jonathan Irwin, Paddy & Gina Johnson, Yoland & Allan Johnson, Art Kavanagh, Sean Keane, Mark Kennedy, Seosamh Lalor, LeAnne Lawton-Tancred, John Frances & Jayne Lieber, Richard & Beatrice Lombard, Pat McCabe, Vinny Jasper McCarthy, William & Emily McClintock Bunbury, Sylvia McClintock, Stevo McFarland, Annie McGinn, Liam & Winnie McGrath, Paul McLaughlin, Nick McNicholas, Miriam Moore, The Morgan Bar (The Morgan Hotel), Tony Mullen, Patsey Murphy, Niall Nelligan, Andrew Nolan, Oisin Nolan Solicitors, Robert O'Byrne, Margaret O'Loghlen, Atalanta Pollock, Paul E. Price, Chris & Ellie Pringle, Richard & Jenny Pringle, Pubspy (*Sunday World*), Ben & Jessica Rathdonnell, John Rogers, Sonia Rogers, Anna-Maija & Erkko Ruohoniemi, Patrick & Christine Ryall, Ronan Sheehan, Olaf & Anna-Marie Shiel,Paul Smith, Jack Teeling, Humphry Wakefield, Sam & Phil Ware, Tony Whelan, John Wilkinson, Jane Williams, Marcus & Olga Williams, Ingo, Stella & Caio Worbs.